British Railway Atlas

M. G. BALL

4TH EDITION

Front cover Class 465/1 Networker No 465196 approaches Waterloo East on 31 May 2012, forming the 09.39 Southeastern service from Charing Cross to Gillingham, via Woolwich Arsenal. *Brian Morrison*

First published 1995
Second edition 1998
3rd Edition 2004
4th Edition 2014

ISBN 978 0 7110 3803 5

© Ian Allan Publishing 2014

Published by Ian Allan Publishing

an imprint of Ian Allan Publishing Ltd, Hersham, Surrey KT12 4RG.
Printed in England

Visit the Ian Allan Publishing website at www.ianallanpublishing.com

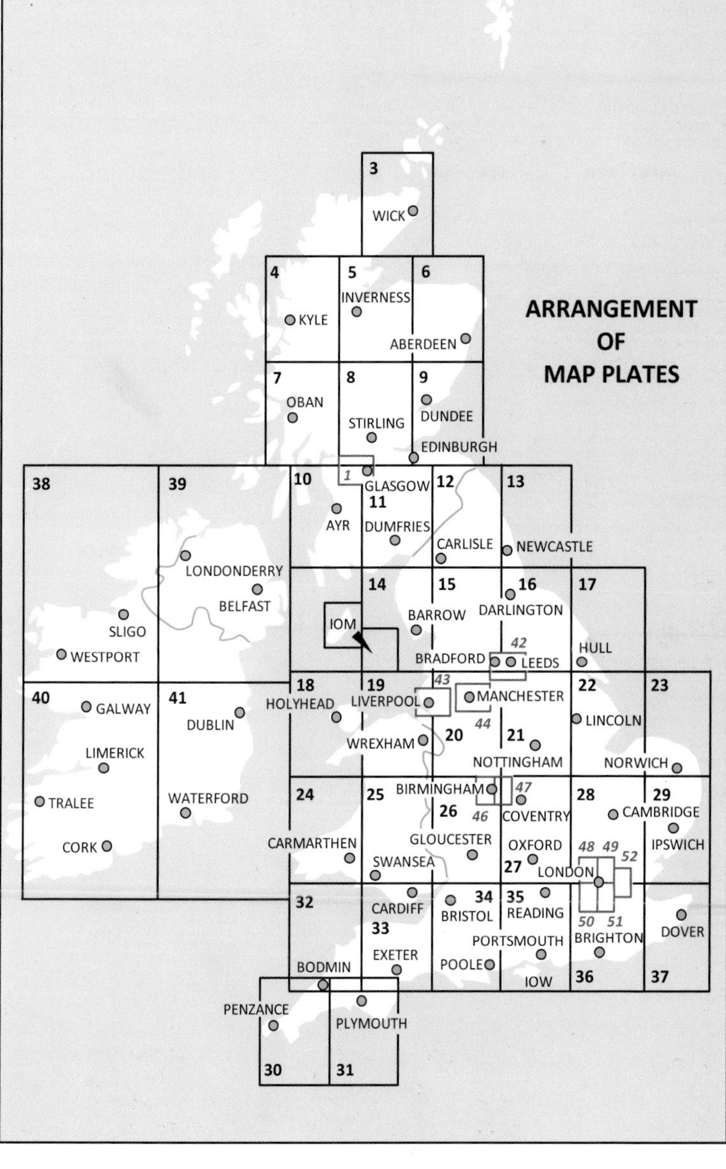

ARRANGEMENT OF MAP PLATES

3 WICK

4 KYLE

5 INVERNESS

6 ABERDEEN

7 OBAN

8 STIRLING

9 DUNDEE

EDINBURGH

1 GLASGOW

10

11 AYR DUMFRIES

12 CARLISLE

13 NEWCASTLE

38

39 LONDONDERRY BELFAST

SLIGO WESTPORT

14 IOM

15 BARROW

16 DARLINGTON

17 HULL

42 BRADFORD LEEDS

40 GALWAY

LIMERICK

TRALEE

CORK

41 DUBLIN

WATERFORD

18 HOLYHEAD

19 LIVERPOOL

43

20 WREXHAM

44 MANCHESTER

21 NOTTINGHAM

22 LINCOLN

23 NORWICH

24 CARMARTHEN

25 BIRMINGHAM

SWANSEA

26 GLOUCESTER

46 *47* COVENTRY

27 OXFORD LONDON

28

48 *49* *52*

CAMBRIDGE

29 IPSWICH

32 CARDIFF

33 EXETER

BODMIN

34 BRISTOL

35 READING

PORTSMOUTH POOLE

IOW

50 *51* BRIGHTON

36

DOVER

37

30 PENZANCE

31 PLYMOUTH

Key to Atlas

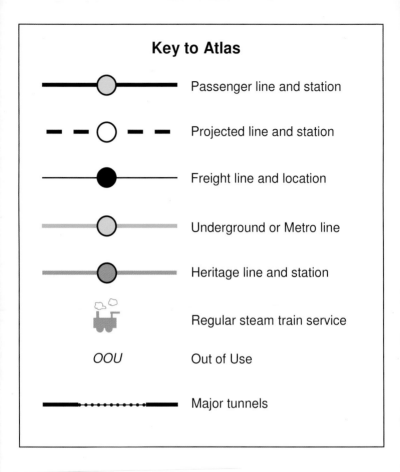

Passenger line and station

Projected line and station

Freight line and location

Underground or Metro line

Heritage line and station

Regular steam train service

OOU   Out of Use

Major tunnels

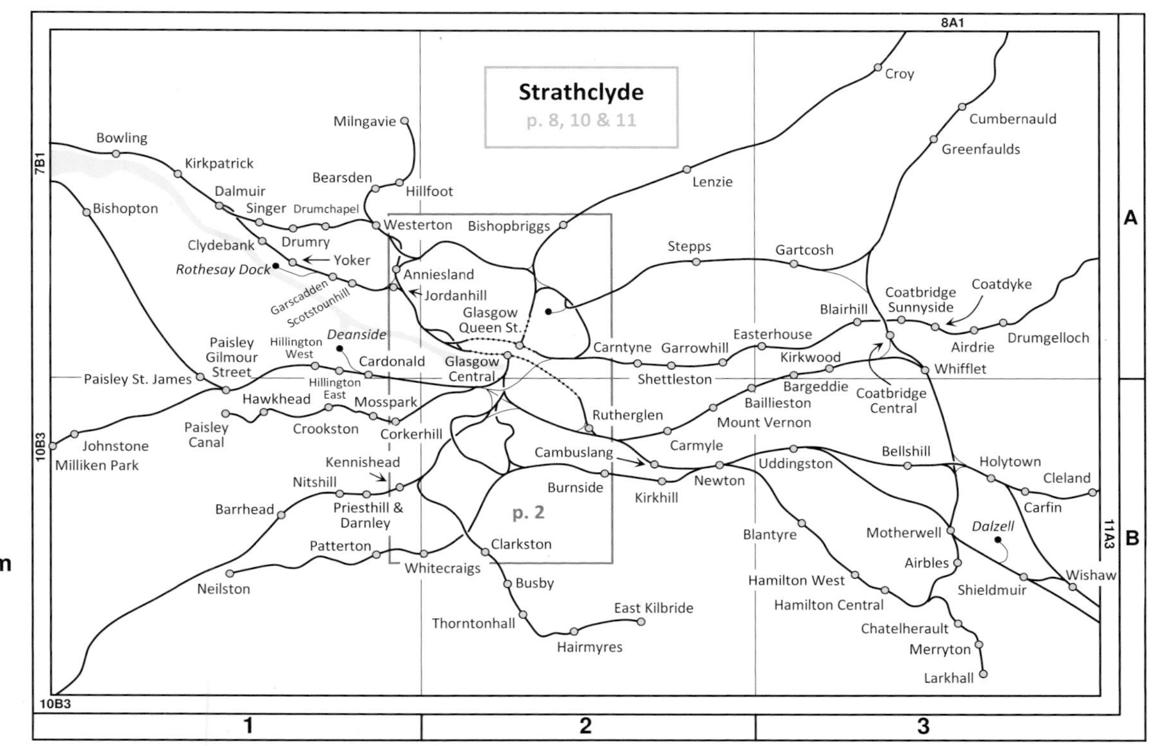

Strathclyde
p. 8, 10 & 11

A

B

8A1

11A3

7B1

10B3

Cumbernauld
Greenfaulds
Croy
Lenzie
Gartcosh
Stepps
Bishopbriggs
Westerton
Hillfoot
Milngavie
Bearsden
Dalmuir
Kirkpatrick
Bowling
Bishopton
Singer
Drumchapel
Drumry
Yoker
Rothesay Dock
Scotstounhill
Clydebank
Deanside
Anniesland
Jordanhill
Glasgow Queen St.
Cardonald
Hillington West
Hillington East
Mosspark
Corkerhill
Glasgow Central
Paisley Gilmour Street
Paisley Canal
Paisley St. James
Johnstone
Milliken Park
Hawkhead
Crookston
Nitshill
Kennishead
Priesthill & Darnley
Barrhead
Neilston
Patterton
Whitecraigs
Thornton hall
Busby
Clarkston
Hairmyres
East Kilbride
Drumgelloch
Coatdyke
Airdrie
Whifflet
Coatbridge Sunnyside
Blairhill
Kirkhill
Easterhouse
Garrowhill
Carntyne
Shettleston
Carmyle
Rutherglen
Cambuslang
Burnside
Kirkhill
Newton
p. 2
Holytown
Cleland
Carfin
Wishaw
Shieldmuir
Dalzell
Motherwell
Airbles
Merryton
Larkhall
Chatelherault
Hamilton Central
Hamilton West
Uddingston
Blantyre
Bellshill
Coatbridge Central
Bargeddie
Baillieston
Mount Vernon

```
M 4
  3
  2
  1
  0
  2
  4
  6  km
```

1

3

2

1

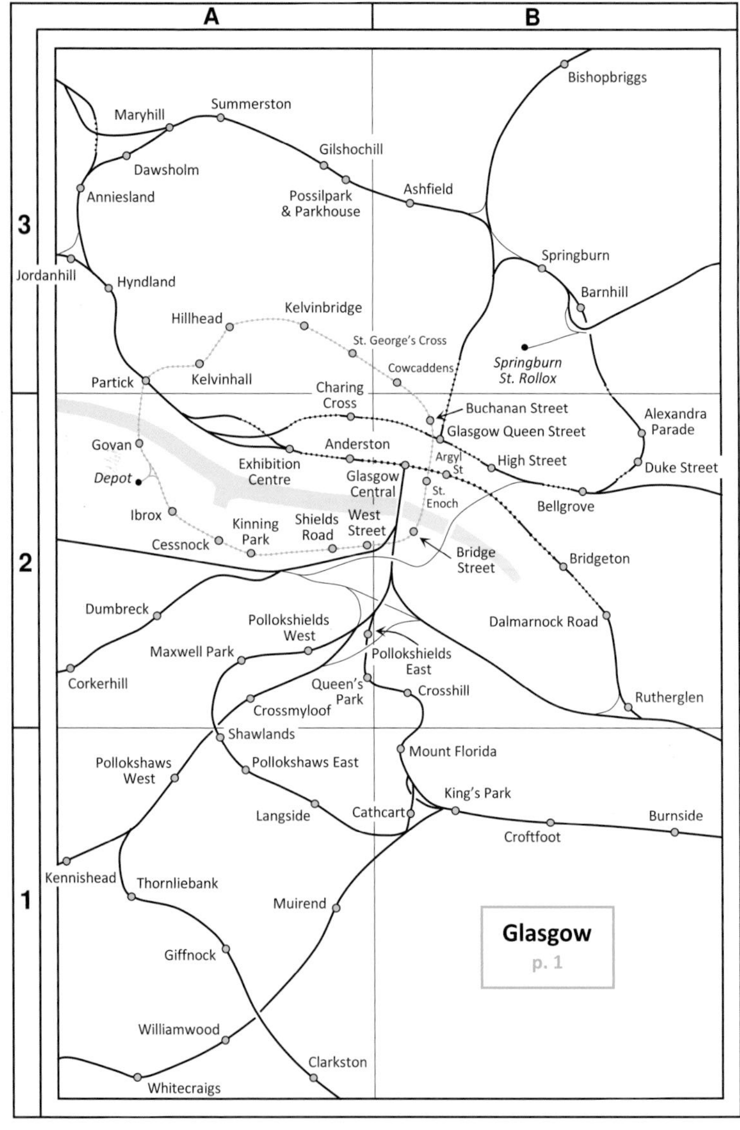
A
B
3
2
1
Bishopbriggs
Summerston
Maryhill
Gilshochill
Dawsholm
Possilpark
& Parkhouse
Ashfield
Anniesland
Springburn
Jordanhill
Hyndland
Barnhill
Kelvinbridge
Hillhead
St. George's Cross
Springburn
St. Rollox
Cowcaddens
Kelvinhall
Partick
Charing
Cross
Buchanan Street
Alexandra
Parade
Glasgow Queen Street
Govan
Anderston
Argyl
St
High Street
Duke Street
Exhibition
Centre
Glasgow
Central
Depot
St.
Enoch
Bellgrove
Ibrox
West
Street
Kinning
Park
Shields
Road
Bridge
Street
Cessnock
Bridgeton
Dumbreck
Pollokshields
West
Dalmarnock Road
Maxwell Park
Pollokshields
East
Corkerhill
Queen's
Park
Crosshill
Rutherglen
Crossmyloof
Shawlands
Mount Florida
Pollokshaws
West
Pollokshaws East
King's Park
Langside
Cathcart
Burnside
Croftfoot
Kennishead
Thornliebank
Muirend
Glasgow
p. 1
Giffnock
Williamwood
Clarkston
Whitecraigs

M 1 0 1 2 km

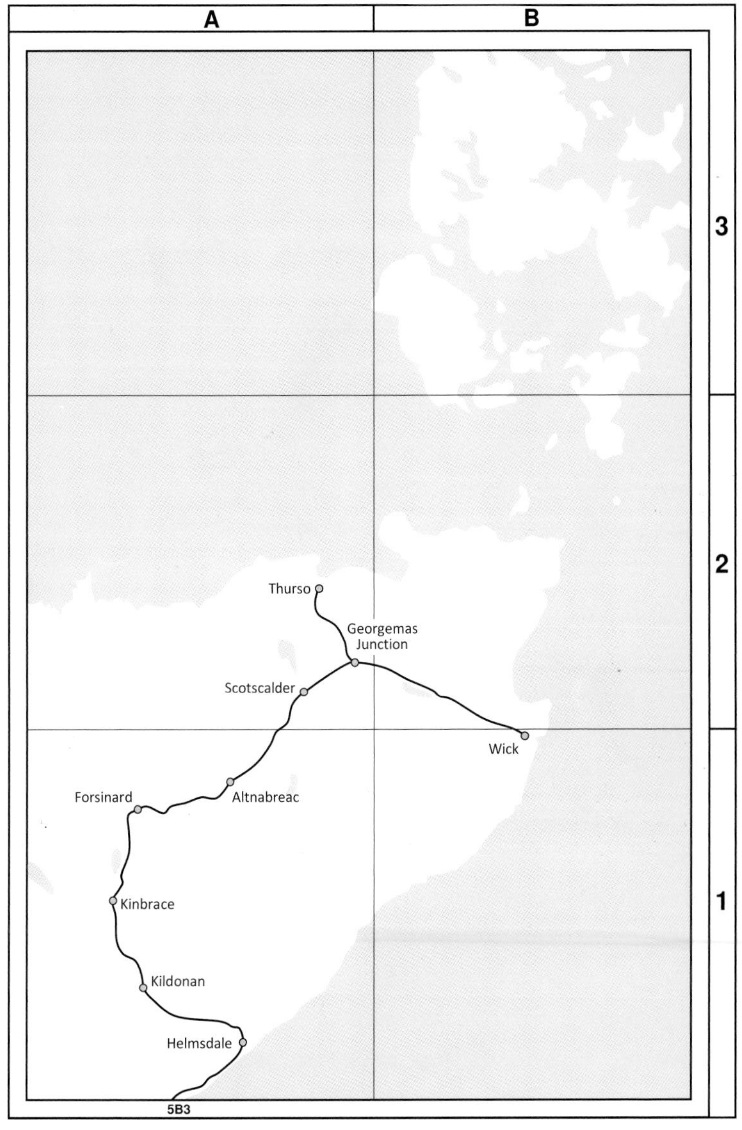

A | B

3

2

1

Thurso

Georgemas
Junction

Scotscalder

Wick

Forsinard | Altnabreac

Kinbrace

Kildonan

Helmsdale

5B3

M 15 10 5 0 5 10 15 20 km

3

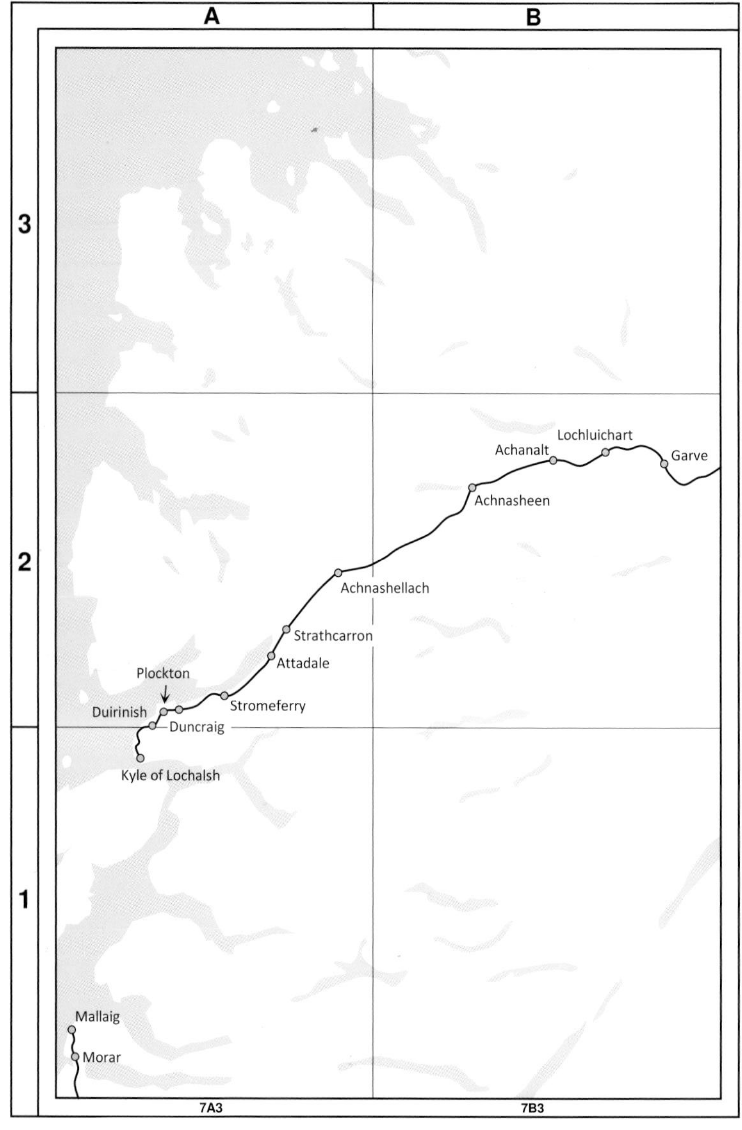

	A	B
3		
2		
1		

Lochluichart
Achanalt
Garve
Achnasheen
Achnashellach
Strathcarron
Plockton
Attadale
Duirinish
Stromeferry
Duncraig
Kyle of Lochalsh
Mallaig
Morar

7A3
7B3

4

M 15 10 5 0 5 10 15 20 km

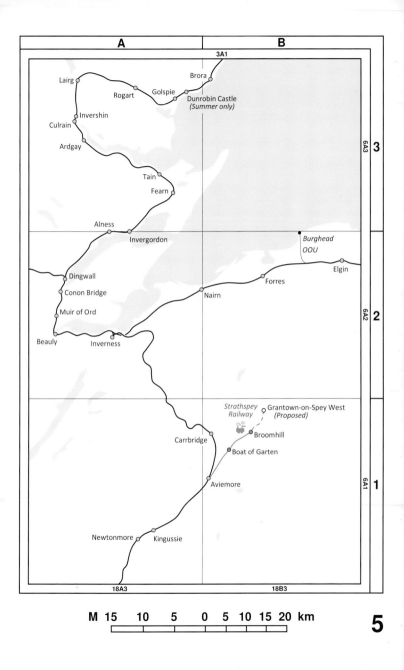
A
B
3A1
Lairg
Brora
Rogart
Golspie
Dunrobin Castle
(Summer only)
Invershin
Culrain
Ardgay
Tain
Fearn
Alness
Invergordon
Burghead
OOU
Elgin
Dingwall
Forres
Conon Bridge
Nairn
Muir of Ord
Beauly
Inverness
Strathspey
Railway
Grantown-on-Spey West
(Proposed)
Broomhill
Carrbridge
Boat of Garten
Aviemore
Newtonmore
Kingussie
18A3
18B3
6A3
3
6A2
2
6A1
1
M 15 10 5 0 5 10 15 20 km

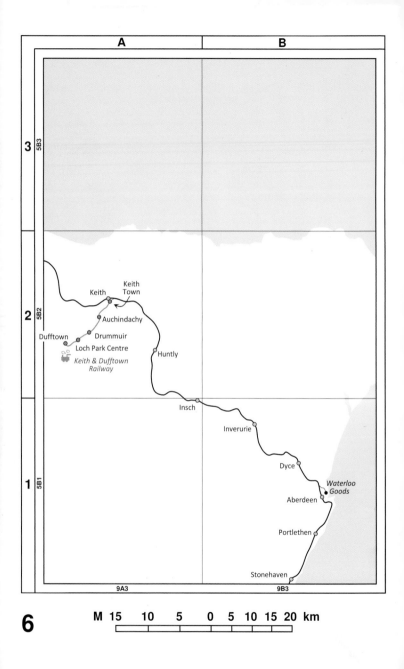

	A	B
3	5B3	
2	5B2	
1	5B1	

Keith
Keith Town
Auchindachy
Dufftown
Drummuir
Loch Park Centre
Keith & Dufftown Railway
Huntly
Insch
Inverurie
Dyce
Waterloo Goods
Aberdeen
Portlethen
Stonehaven

9A3   9B3

M 15 10 5 0 5 10 15 20 km

6

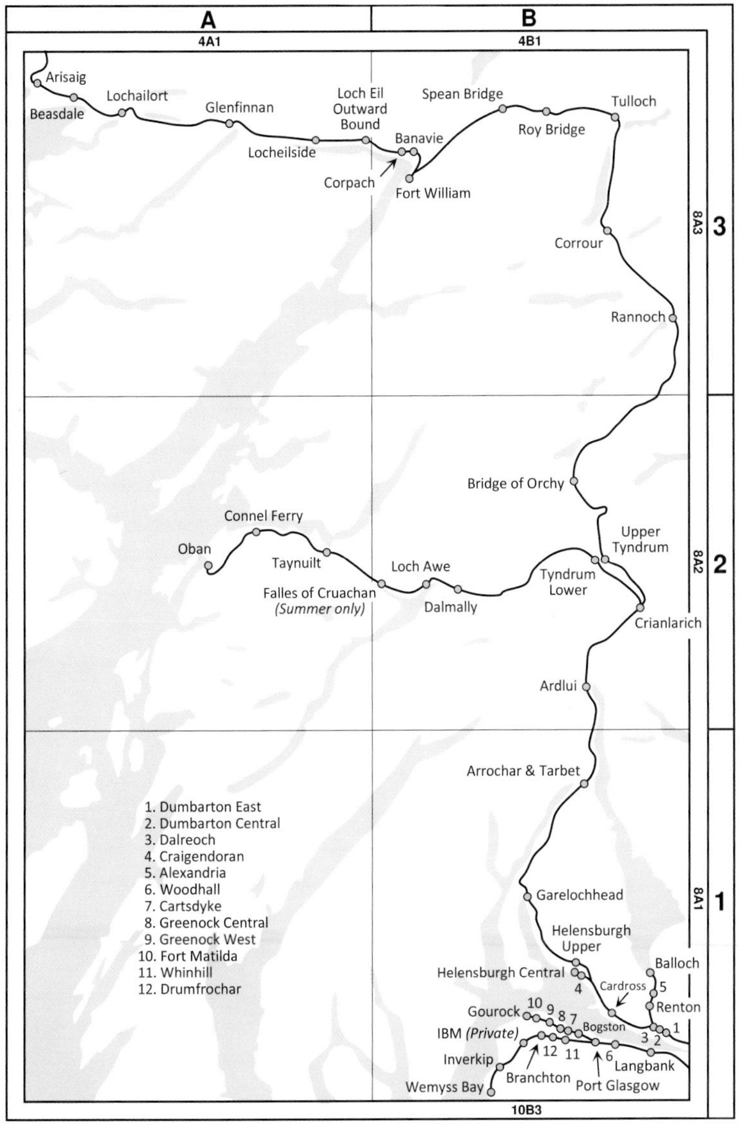

Arisaig
Lochailort
Beasdale
Glenfinnan
Loch Eil Outward Bound
Locheilside
Spean Bridge
Tulloch
Banavie
Roy Bridge
Corpach
Fort William

Corrour

Rannoch

Bridge of Orchy

Connel Ferry

Upper Tyndrum

Oban
Taynuilt
Loch Awe
Tyndrum Lower
Falles of Cruachan
(Summer only)
Dalmally
Crianlarich

Ardlui

Arrochar & Tarbet

Garelochhead

Helensburgh Upper

Balloch

Helensburgh Central
Cardross
4
Renton
5

Gourock
10 9 8 7
Bogston
IBM (Private)
12 11 6
3 2 1
Inverkip
Branchton
Langbank
Wemyss Bay
Port Glasgow

1. Dumbarton East
2. Dumbarton Central
3. Dalreoch
4. Craigendoran
5. Alexandria
6. Woodhall
7. Cartsdyke
8. Greenock Central
9. Greenock West
10. Fort Matilda
11. Whinhill
12. Drumfrochar

M 15 10 5 0 5 10 15 20 km

7

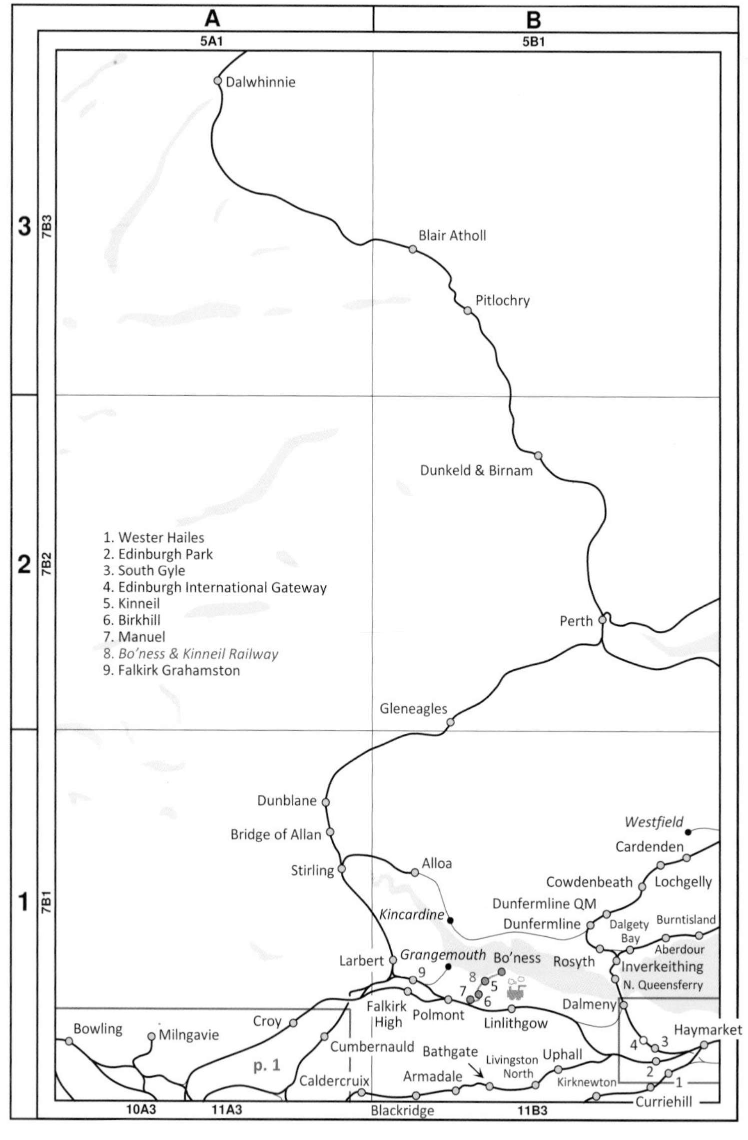

	A	**B**	
	5A1	5B1	

1. Wester Hailes
2. Edinburgh Park
3. South Gyle
4. Edinburgh International Gateway
5. Kinneil
6. Birkhill
7. Manuel
8. *Bo'ness & Kinneil Railway*
9. Falkirk Grahamston

Dalwhinnie

Blair Atholl

Pitlochry

Dunkeld & Birnam

Perth

Gleneagles

Dunblane

Bridge of Allan

Stirling

Alloa

Kincardine

Larbert

Grangemouth

Bo'ness

Westfield

Cardenden

Cowdenbeath

Lochgelly

Dunfermline QM

Dunfermline

Dalgety Bay

Burntisland

Aberdour

Rosyth

Inverkeithing

N. Queensferry

Dalmeny

Bowling

Milngavie

Croy

Falkirk High

Polmont

Linlithgow

Uphall

Haymarket

Cumbernauld

Bathgate

Livingston North

Kirknewton

Currie hill

Caldercruix

Armadale

p. 1

10A3 | 11A3 | Blackridge | 11B3

8

M 15 10 5 0 5 10 15 20 km

7B3 | 7B2 | 7B1

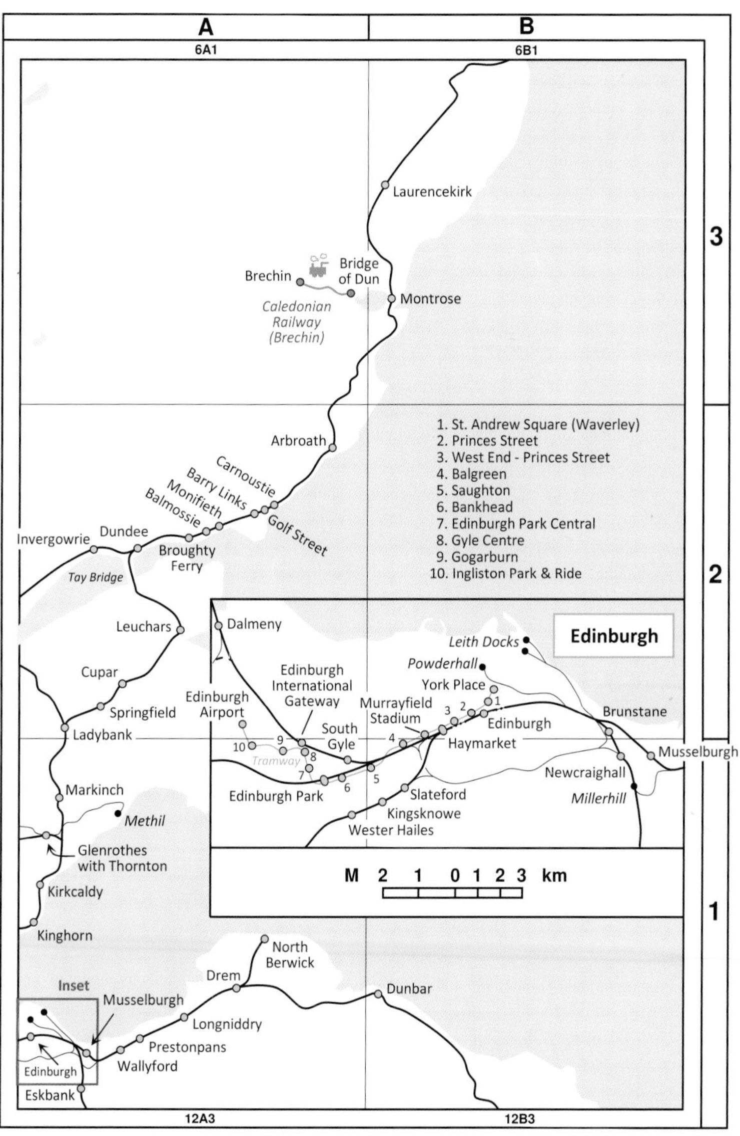

	A	B	
	6A1	6B1	

3

Laurencekirk

Brechin — Bridge of Dun

Caledonian Railway (Brechin)

Montrose

Arbroath

1. St. Andrew Square (Waverley)
2. Princes Street
3. West End - Princes Street
4. Balgreen
5. Saughton
6. Bankhead
7. Edinburgh Park Central
8. Gyle Centre
9. Gogarburn
10. Ingliston Park & Ride

Carnoustie
Barry Links
Monifieth
Balmossie
Golf Street

Invergowrie
Dundee
Tay Bridge
Broughty Ferry

2

Dalmeny

Leith Docks

Edinburgh

Powderhall

York Place

Leuchars

Edinburgh International Gateway

Murrayfield Stadium

1

Cupar

Edinburgh Airport

3 2

Brunstane

Springfield

South Gyle

Edinburgh

Ladybank

10 9

Tramway

4

Haymarket

Musselburgh

8

7

5

Newcraighall

Markinch

6

Slateford

Millerhill

Methil

Edinburgh Park

Kingsknowe
Wester Hailes

Glenrothes with Thornton

M 2 1 0 1 2 3 km

Kirkcaldy

Kinghorn

1

North Berwick

Inset

Drem

Musselburgh

Dunbar

Longniddry

Prestonpans

Edinburgh

Wallyford

Eskbank

| 12A3 | 12B3 |

M 15 10 5 0 5 10 15 20 km

9

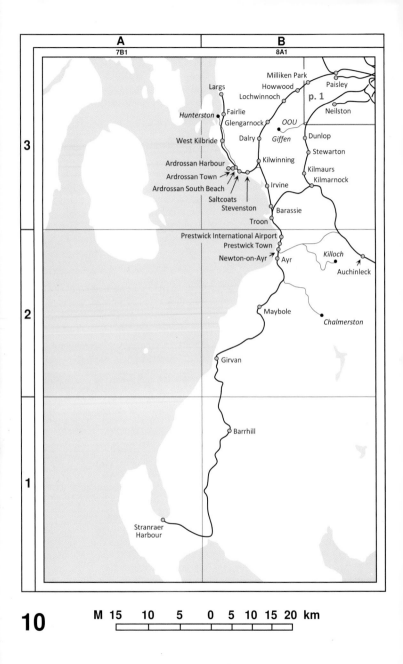

Milliken Park
Howwood
Paisley
Lochwinnoch
Largs
Neilston
Fairlie
Hunterston
Glengarnock
OOU
West Kilbride
Dalry
Giffen
Dunlop
Stewarton
Ardrossan Harbour
Kilwinning
Kilmaurs
Ardrossan Town
Kilmarnock
Ardrossan South Beach
Irvine
Saltcoats
Stevenston
Barassie
Troon
Prestwick International Airport
Prestwick Town
Killoch
Newton-on-Ayr
Ayr
Auchinleck
Maybole
Chalmerston
Girvan
Barrhill
Stranraer
Harbour

p. 1

3

2

1

10

M 15 10 5 0 5 10 15 20 km

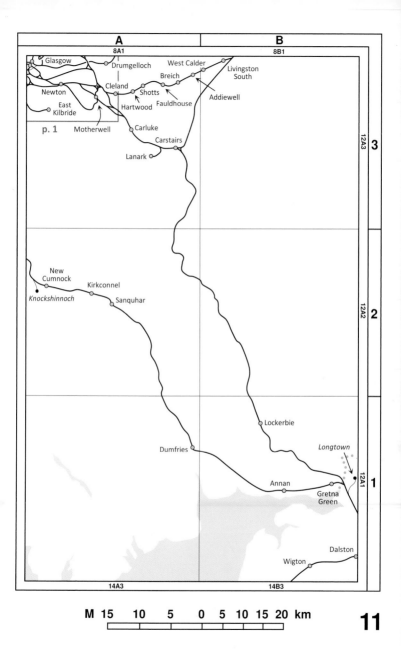

Glasgow

Drumgelloch

West Calder

Breich

Livingston South

Newton

Cleland

Shotts

East Kilbride

Hartwood

Fauldhouse

Addiewell

p. 1

Motherwell

Carluke

Carstairs

Lanark

12A3

New Cumnock

Kirkconnel

Knockshinnoch

Sanquhar

12A2

Lockerbie

Longtown

Dumfries

Annan

Gretna Green

12A1

Dalston

Wigton

M   15   10   5   0   5   10   15   20   km

11

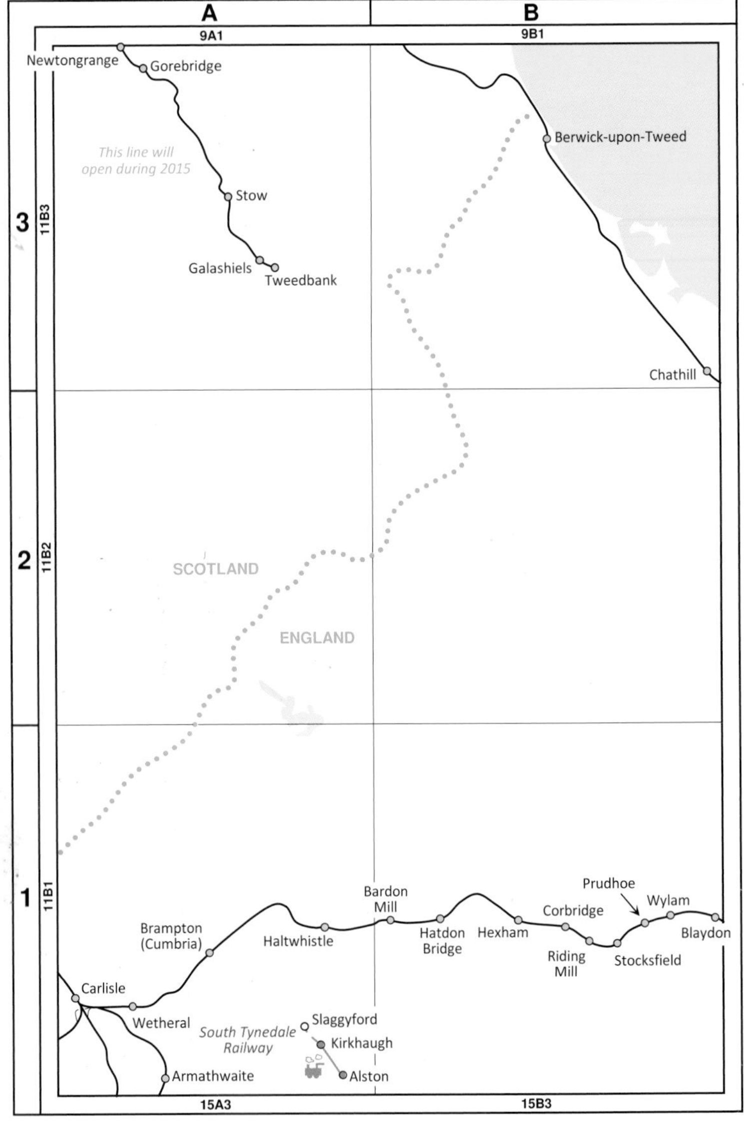

A | B

9A1 | 9B1

Newtongrange ○ Gorebridge

*This line will
open during 2015*

○ Stow

Galashiels ○ Tweedbank

Berwick-upon-Tweed

Chathill

3

11B3

SCOTLAND

ENGLAND

2

11B2

1

11B1

Bardon
Mill

Prudhoe
Wylam

Brampton
(Cumbria)   Haltwhistle   Hatdon   Hexham   Corbridge   Blaydon
                              Bridge   Stocksfield
Carlisle   Riding
                                                Mill
Wetheral   *South Tynedale*   Slaggyford
            Railway   Kirkhaugh
Armathwaite   Alston

15A3 | 15B3

12   M 15   10   5   0   5   10   15   20 km

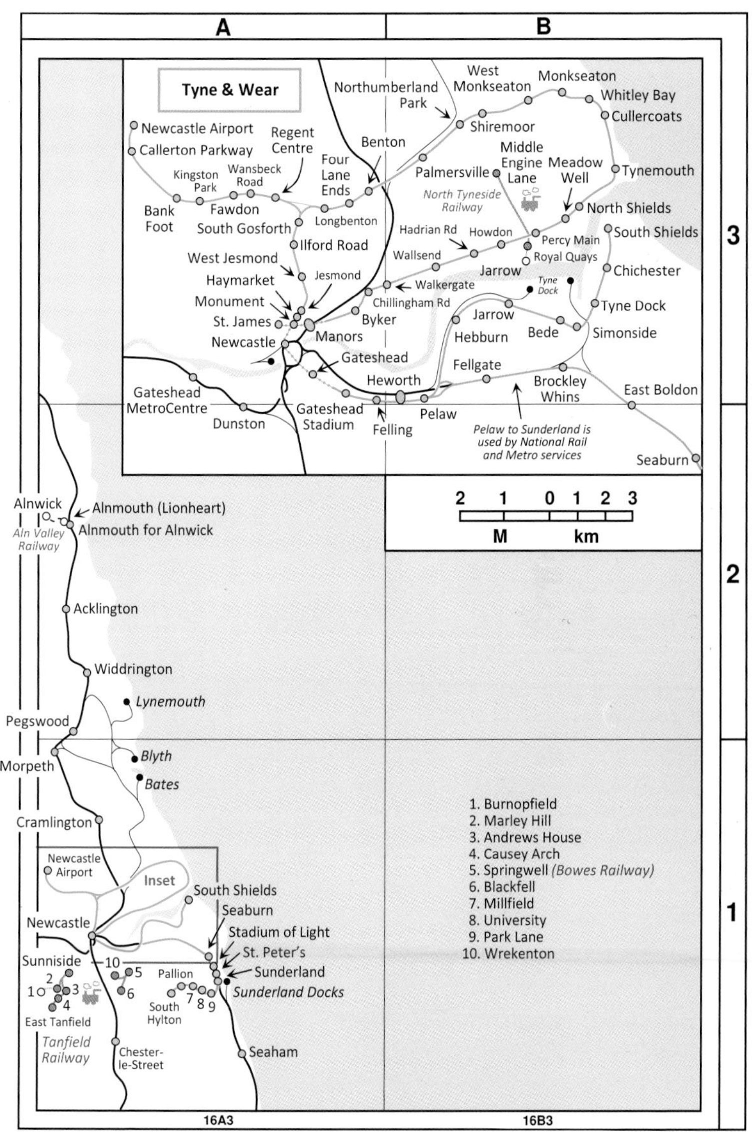

	A	B	

Tyne & Wear

Newcastle Airport
Callerton Parkway
Regent Centre
Northumberland Park
West Monkseaton
Monkseaton
Whitley Bay
Cullercoats
Benton
Shiremoor
Middle Engine Lane
Meadow Well
Tynemouth
Kingston Park
Wansbeck Road
Four Lane Ends
Palmersville
North Tyneside Railway
North Shields
South Shields
Bank Foot
Fawdon
South Gosforth
Longbenton
Hadrian Rd
Howdon
Percy Main
Royal Quays
Chichester
West Jesmond
Ilford Road
Wallsend
Jarrow
Tyne Dock
Haymarket
Jesmond
Walkergate
Tyne Dock
Monument
Chillingham Rd
Jarrow
Simonside
St. James
Byker
Hebburn
Bede
Newcastle
Manors
Gateshead
Fellgate
Gateshead MetroCentre
Heworth
Brockley Whins
East Boldon
Dunston
Gateshead Stadium
Pelaw
Felling

Pelaw to Sunderland is used by National Rail and Metro services

Seaburn

2 1 0 1 2 3
M km

Alnwick
Alnmouth (Lionheart)
Aln Valley Railway
Alnmouth for Alnwick

Acklington

Widdrington

Lynemouth

Pegswood

Blyth

Morpeth

Bates

Cramlington

Newcastle Airport

Inset

Newcastle
South Shields
Seaburn
Stadium of Light
St. Peter's
Sunniside
10
5
Pallion
Sunderland
2
Sunderland Docks
1
3
6
7 8 9
4
South Hylton
East Tanfield
Tanfield Railway
Chester-le-Street
Seaham

1. Burnopfield
2. Marley Hill
3. Andrews House
4. Causey Arch
5. Springwell *(Bowes Railway)*
6. Blackfell
7. Millfield
8. University
9. Park Lane
10. Wrekenton

16A3

16B3

M 15 10 5 0 5 10 15 20 km

13

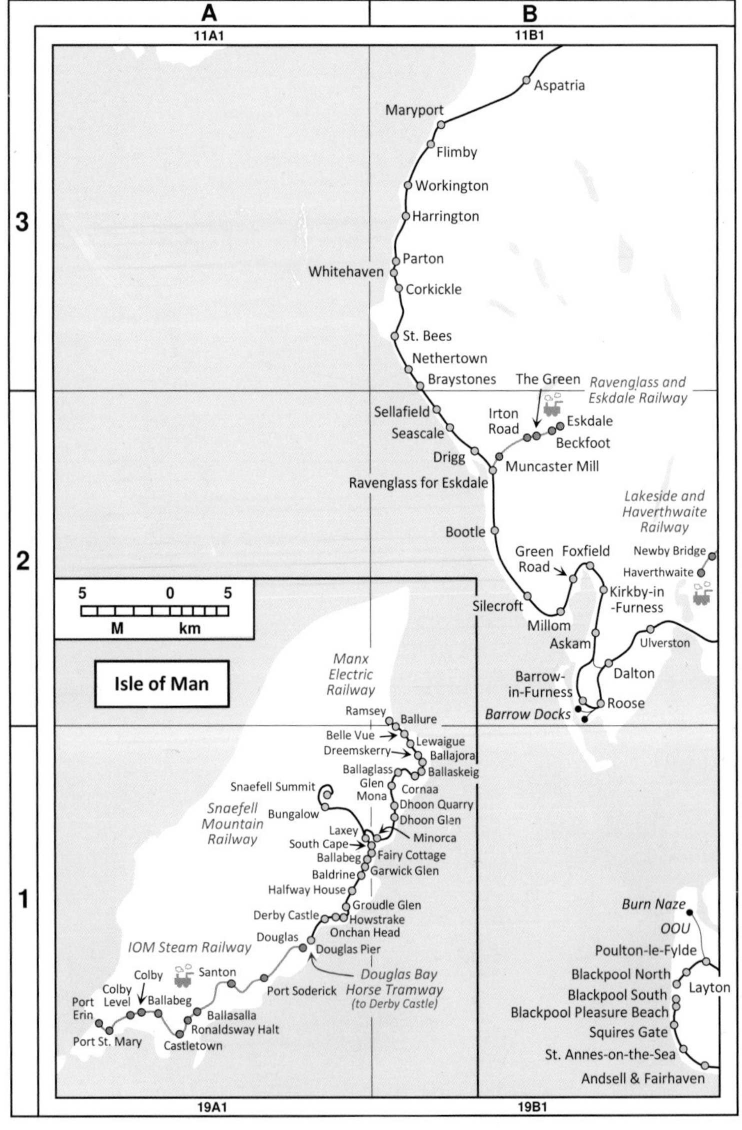

	A	B
	11A1	11B1

3

Aspatria
Maryport
Flimby
Workington
Harrington
Parton
Whitehaven
Corkickle
St. Bees
Nethertown
Braystones
The Green *Ravenglass and Eskdale Railway*

2

Sellafield
Seascale
Irton Road
Eskdale
Beckfoot
Drigg
Muncaster Mill
Ravenglass for Eskdale

Lakeside and Haverthwaite Railway

Bootle
Green Road Foxfield Newby Bridge
Haverthwaite
Kirkby-in-Furness
Silecroft
Millom
Askam Ulverston
Manx Electric Railway
Barrow-in-Furness Dalton
Isle of Man
5 0 5
M km
Barrow Docks Roose

1

Ramsey Ballure
Belle Vue Lewaigue
Dreemskerry Ballajora
Ballaglass Ballaskeig
Snaefell Summit Glen Mona Cornaa
Dhoon Quarry
Snaefell Mountain Railway
Bungalow Dhoon Glen
Laxey Minorca
South Cape Fairy Cottage
Ballabeg Garwick Glen
Baldrine
Halfway House
Derby Castle Groudle Glen
Howstrake
Douglas Onchan Head
Douglas Pier
IOM Steam Railway Port Soderick *Douglas Bay Horse Tramway (to Derby Castle)*
Colby Santon
Port Level Ballabeg
Erin Ballasalla
Port St. Mary Ronaldsway Halt
Castletown

Burn Naze
OOU
Poulton-le-Fylde
Blackpool North
Blackpool South Layton
Blackpool Pleasure Beach
Squires Gate
St. Annes-on-the-Sea
Andsell & Fairhaven

| | 19A1 | 19B1 |

14

M 15 10 5 0 5 10 15 20 km

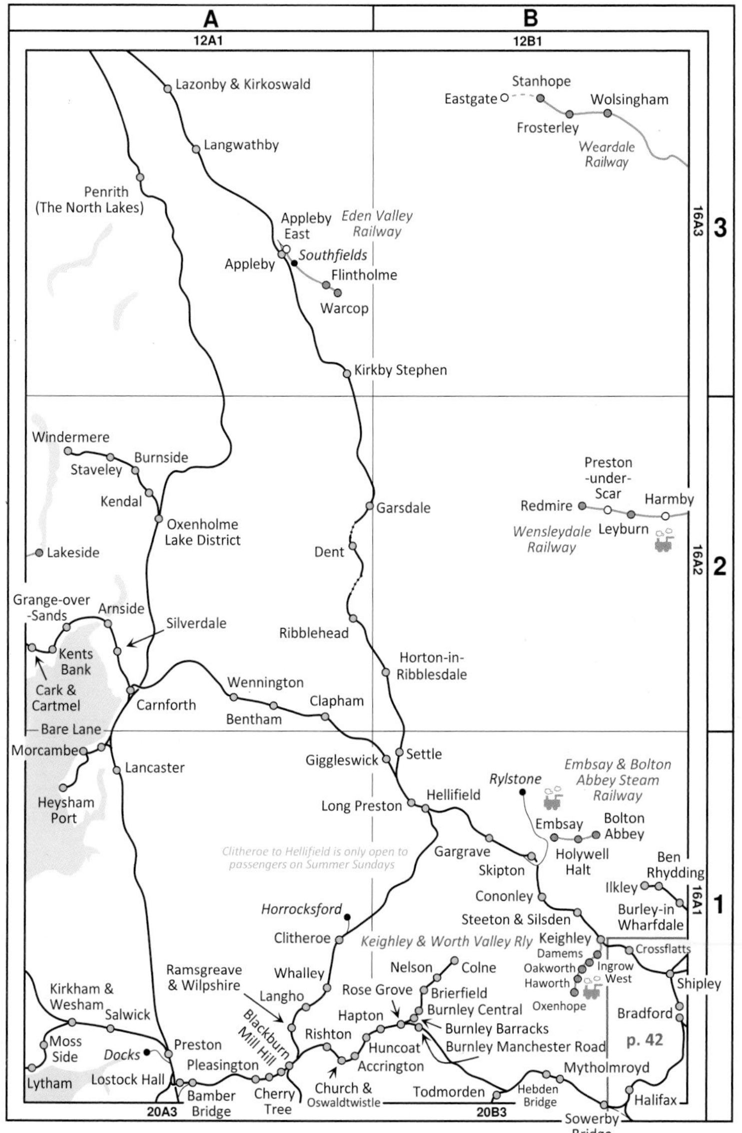

Lazonby & Kirkoswald

Langwathby

Penrith
(The North Lakes)

Appleby
East

*Eden Valley
Railway*

Appleby · *Southfields*

Flintholme

Warcop

Kirkby Stephen

Eastgate ○--○ Stanhope

Frosterley ● ● Wolsingham

*Weardale
Railway*

Windermere

Burnside

Staveley

Kendal

Oxenholme
Lake District

Lakeside

Garsdale

Dent

Preston
-under-
Scar

Redmire ● ● Harmby

Leyburn

*Wensleydale
Railway*

Grange-over
-Sands

Arnside

Silverdale

Kents
Bank

Cark &
Cartmel

Bare Lane

Morcambe

Heysham
Port

Lancaster

Carnforth

Wennington

Bentham

Clapham

Ribblehead

Horton-in-
Ribblesdale

Giggleswick

Settle

Long Preston

Hellifield

*Clitheroe to Hellifield is only open to
passengers on Summer Sundays*

Gargrave

Skipton

Cononley

Steeton & Silsden

Rylstone

*Embsay & Bolton
Abbey Steam
Railway*

Embsay

Holywell
Halt

Bolton
Abbey

Ben
Rhydding

Ilkley

Burley-in
Wharfedale

Horrocksford

Clitheroe

Keighley & Worth Valley Rly

Keighley

Crossflatts

Kirkham &
Wesham

Salwick

Moss
Side

Docks

Lytham

Ramsgreave
& Wilpshire

Whalley

Langho

*Blackburn
Mill Hill*

Preston

Pleasington

Lostock Hall

Bamber
Bridge

Cherry
Tree

Nelson

Colne

Rose Grove

Brierfield

Hapton

Rishton

Huncoat

Accrington

Church &
Oswaldtwistle

Burnley Central

Burnley Barracks

Burnley Manchester Road

Todmorden

Damems

Oakworth

Haworth

Oxenhope

Ingrow
West

Shipley

Bradford

Mytholmroyd

Hebden
Bridge

Sowerby
Bridge

Halifax

p. 42

M 15 10 5 0 5 10 15 20 km

15

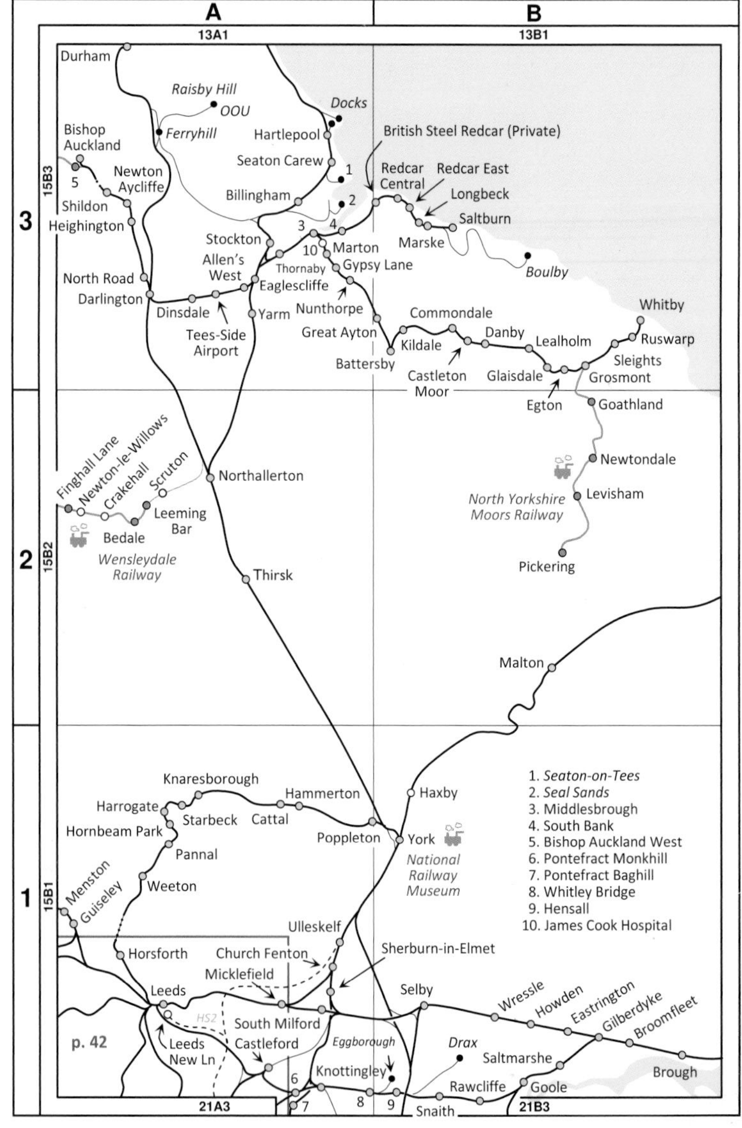

A | B

Durham

Raisby Hill
OOU
Ferryhill

Bishop
Auckland
Newton
Aycliffe

Shildon
Heighington

Docks

Hartlepool

Seaton Carew

Billingham

British Steel Redcar (Private)

1

Redcar
Central
Redcar East
Longbeck
Saltburn

2

3
4
10
Marton
Thornaby
Gypsy Lane
Marske

Boulby

North Road
Darlington

Stockton
Allen's
West
Eaglescliffe
Nunthorpe

Dinsdale
Yarm

Commondale
Danby
Lealholm
Whitby

Tees-Side
Airport

Great Ayton
Kildale
Glaisdale
Ruswarp

Battersby
Castleton
Moor
Egton
Sleights
Grosmont

Goathland

Finghall Lane
Newton-le-Willows
Crakehall
Scruton

Northallerton

Newtondale

Leeming
Bar

Bedale

*North Yorkshire
Moors Railway*

Levisham

*Wensleydale
Railway*

Thirsk

Pickering

Malton

Knaresborough
Hammerton

Haxby

Harrogate

Starbeck
Cattal

Hornbeam Park

Pannal

Poppleton

York

*National
Railway
Museum*

Menston
Guiseley

Weeton

1. *Seaton-on-Tees*
2. *Seal Sands*
3. Middlesbrough
4. South Bank
5. Bishop Auckland West
6. Pontefract Monkhill
7. Pontefract Baghill
8. Whitley Bridge
9. Hensall
10. James Cook Hospital

Horsforth

Ulleskelf

Church Fenton
Micklefield

Sherburn-in-Elmet

Leeds

HS2

Selby
Wressle
Howden
Eastrington
Gilberdyke
Broomfleet

p. 42

Leeds
New Ln
South Milford
Castleford

Eggborough
Drax
Saltmarshe

Brough

6
Knottingley
Rawcliffe
Goole

7
8
9
Snaith

15B3
15B2
15B1

16

M 15 10 5 0 5 10 15 20 km

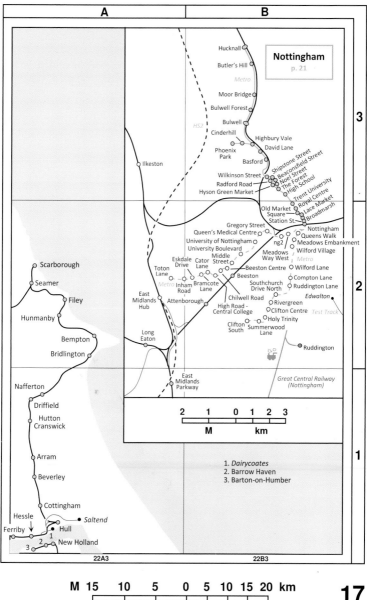

Hucknall

Butler's Hill

Metro

Nottingham
p. 21

Moor Bridge

Bulwell Forest

HS2

Bulwell

Cinderhill

Highbury Vale

David Lane

Phoenix Park

Basford

Ilkeston

Shipstone Street

Beaconsfield Street

Wilkinson Street

Noel Street

Radford Road

The Forest

Hyson Green Market

High School

Trent University

Royal Centre

Old Market Square

Lace Market

Station St.

Broadmarsh

Gregory Street

Nottingham

Queen's Medical Centre

Queens Walk

University of Nottingham

Meadows Embankment

University Boulevard

ng2

Wilford Village

Meadows Way West

Eskdale Drive

Cator Lane

Middle Street

Toton Lane

Beeston Centre

Metro

Wilford Lane

Inham Road

Bramcote Lane

Beeston

Compton Lane

East Midlands Hub

Southchurch Drive North

Ruddington Lane

Attenborough

Chilwell Road

Edwalton

High Road - Central College

Rivergreen

Test Track

Long Eaton

Clifton Centre

Clifton South

Holy Trinity

Summerwood Lane

Ruddington

East Midlands Parkway

Great Central Railway (Nottingham)

Scarborough

Seamer

Filey

Hunmanby

Bempton

Bridlington

Nafferton

Driffield

Hutton Cranswick

Arram

Beverley

Cottingham

Hessle

Saltend

Ferriby

Hull

New Holland

2 1 0 1 2 3

M   km

1. *Dairycoates*
2. Barrow Haven
3. Barton-on-Humber

M 15   10   5   0   5   10   15   20 km

17

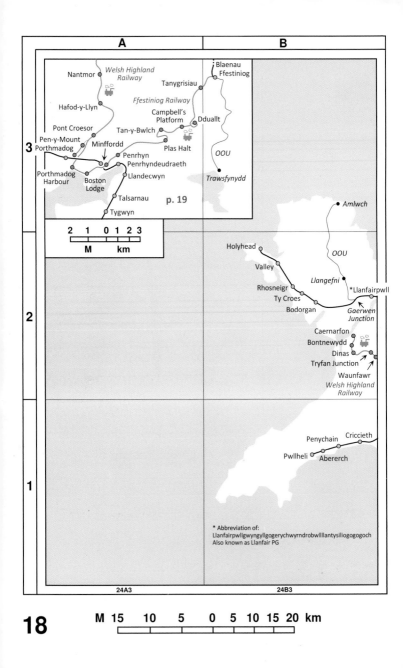

Welsh Highland Railway
Nantmor
Hafod-y-Llyn
Pont Croesor
Pen-y-Mount
Porthmadog
Porthmadog Harbour
Minffordd
Boston Lodge
Penrhyn
Penrhyndeudraeth
Llandecwyn
Talsarnau
Tygwyn

Ffestiniog Railway
Tanygrisiau
Campbell's Platform
Tan-y-Bwlch
Plas Halt
Dduallt
Blaenau Ffestiniog

OOU
Trawsfynydd

p. 19

2 1 0 1 2 3
M   km

Amlwch

OOU

Holyhead
Valley
Llangefni
Rhosneigr
Ty Croes
Bodorgan
*Llanfairpwll
Gaerwen Junction

Caernarfon
Bontnewydd
Dinas
Tryfan Junction
Waunfawr
Welsh Highland Railway

Penychain   Criccieth
Pwllheli   Abererch

* Abbreviation of:
Llanfairpwllgwyngyllgogerychwyrndrobwllllantysiliogogogoch
Also known as Llanfair PG

24A3   24B3

M 15 10 5 0 5 10 15 20 km

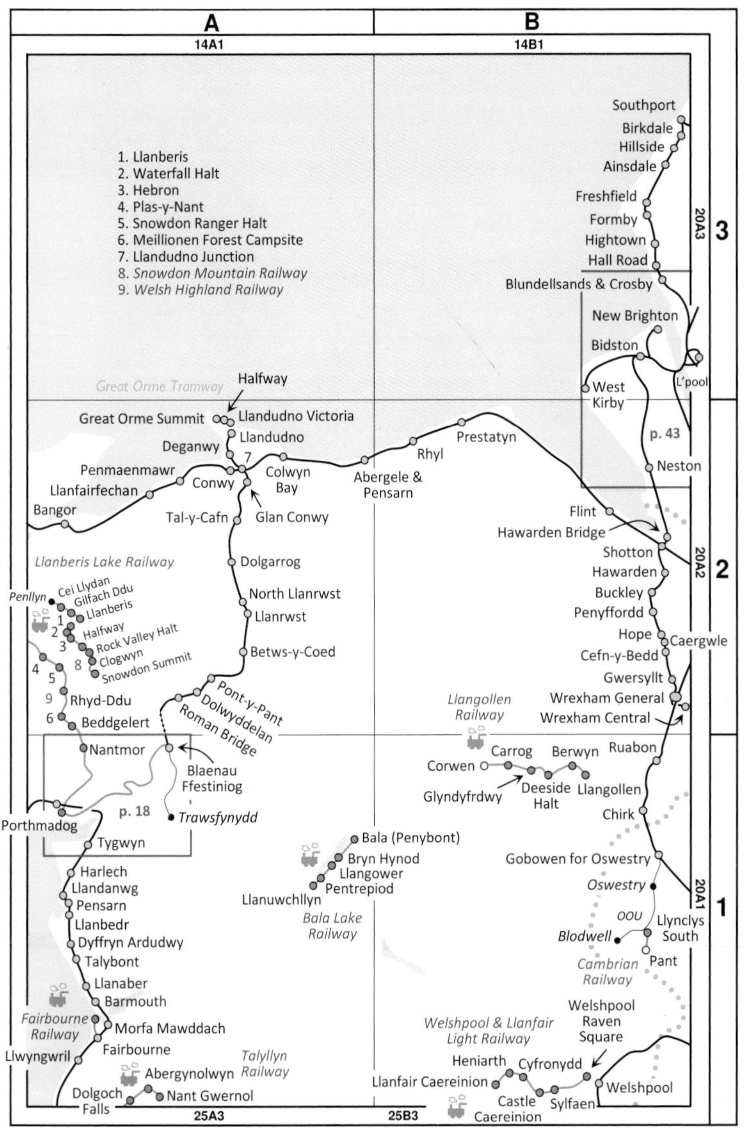

	A	B
	14A1	14B1

1. Llanberis
2. Waterfall Halt
3. Hebron
4. Plas-y-Nant
5. Snowdon Ranger Halt
6. Meillionen Forest Campsite
7. Llandudno Junction
8. *Snowdon Mountain Railway*
9. *Welsh Highland Railway*

Southport
Birkdale
Hillside
Ainsdale
Freshfield
Formby
Hightown
Hall Road
Blundellsands & Crosby
New Brighton
Bidston
L'pool
West Kirby

20A3

Great Orme Tramway Halfway
Great Orme Summit Llandudno Victoria
Deganwy Llandudno
Penmaenmawr 7 Colwyn Bay
Llanfairfechan Conwy Glan Conwy
Bangor Tal-y-Cafn

Prestatyn
Rhyl
Abergele & Pensarn

p. 43

Neston

Flint
Hawarden Bridge
Shotton
Hawarden
Buckley
Penyffordd
Hope
Caergwle
Cefn-y-Bedd
Gwersyllt
Wrexham General
Wrexham Central

20A2

Llanberis Lake Railway
Penllyn Cei Llydan
Gilfach Ddu
Llanberis
Halfway
Rock Valley Halt
Clogwyn
Snowdon Summit
Rhyd-Ddu
Beddgelert
Nantmor
Blaenau Ffestiniog
p. 18 *Trawsfynydd*

Dolgarrog
North Llanrwst
Llanrwst
Betws-y-Coed
Pont-y-Pant
Dolwyddelan
Roman Bridge

Llangollen Railway
Carrog Berwyn
Corwen Ruabon
Glyndyfrdwy Deeside Halt Llangollen
Chirk

20A1

Porthmadog
Tygwyn
Harlech
Llandanwg
Pensarn
Llanbedr
Dyffryn Ardudwy
Talybont
Llanaber
Barmouth
Fairbourne Railway
Morfa Mawddach
Llwyngwril Fairbourne
Abergynolwyn
Dolgoch Falls Nant Gwernol
Talyllyn Railway

Bala (Penybont)
Bryn Hynod
Llangower
Pentrepiod
Llanuwchllyn
Bala Lake Railway

Gobowen for Oswestry
Oswestry
OOU
Llynclys South
Blodwell Pant
Cambrian Railway

Welshpool Raven Square
Welshpool & Llanfair Light Railway
Heniarth Cyfronydd
Llanfair Caereinion Welshpool
Castle Sylfaen
Caereinion

| 25A3 | 25B3 |

M 15   10   5   0   5   10   15   20 km

19

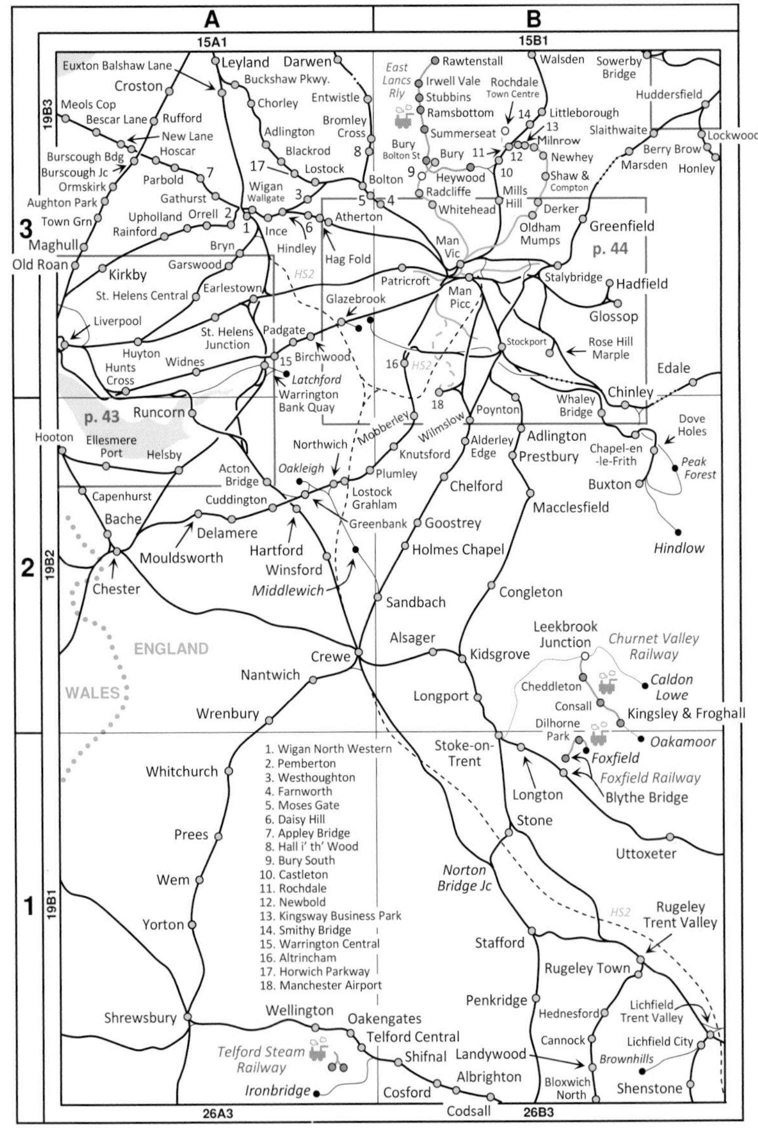

A 15A1   B 15B1

p. 43
p. 44

19B3

Euxton Balshaw Lane
Meols Cop
Bescar Lane
Croston
Leyland
Darwen
Buckshaw Pkwy.
Chorley
Rufford
New Lane
Hoscar
Adlington
Blackrod
Bromley Cross
Entwistle
East Lancs Rly
Rawtenstall
Walsden
Sowerby Bridge
Huddersfield
Slaithwaite
Lockwood
Irwell Vale
Stubbins
Ramsbottom
Rochdale Town Centre
Littleborough
Summerseat
Milnrow
Newhey
Marsden
Berry Brow
Honley
Burscough Bdg
Burscough Jc
Ormskirk
Parbold
Gathurst
Aughton Park
Town Grn
Rainford
Kirkby
Garswood
St. Helens Central
Liverpool
Huyton
Hunts Cross
Widnes
Wigan Wallgate
Upholland
Orrell
Ince
Hindley
Bryn
Earlestown
St. Helens Junction
Padgate
Birchwood
Latchford
Warrington Bank Quay
Bolton St.
Bury
Heywood
Radcliffe
Whitehead
Bury South
Man Vic
Shaw & Compton
Oldham Mumps
Derker
Greenfield
Hadfield
Glossop
Rose Hill Marple
Edale
Hag Fold
Atherton
Patricroft
Man Picc
Stockport
Stalybridge
Whaley Bridge
Chinley
Dove Holes
Peak Forest
Buxton
Hindlow
HS2
Glazebrook
Old Roan
Hooton
Ellesmere Port
Helsby
Capenhurst
Bache
Chester
Delamere
Mouldsworth
Acton Bridge
Cuddington
Hartford
Winsford
Middlewich
Sandbach
Oakleigh
Northwich
Lostock Graham
Plumley
Greenbank
Holmes Chapel
Knutsford
Alderley Edge
Chelford
Goostrey
Prestbury
Adlington
Macclesfield
Chapel-en-le-Frith
Mobberley
Wilmslow
Poynton
ENGLAND
WALES
Runcorn
Crewe
Nantwich
Wrenbury
Whitchurch
Prees
Wem
Yorton
Shrewsbury
Alsager
Kidsgrove
Longport
Crewe
Congleton
Leekbrook Junction
Churnet Valley Railway
Cheddleton
Consall
Dilhorne Park
Caldon Lowe
Kingsley & Froghall
Oakamoor
Foxfield
Foxfield Railway
Blythe Bridge
Stoke-on-Trent
Longton
Stone
Uttoxeter
Norton Bridge Jc
HS2
Rugeley Trent Valley
Stafford
Rugeley Town
Penkridge
Hednesford
Cannock
Lichfield Trent Valley
Lichfield City
Brownhills
Shenstone
Wellington
Oakengates
Telford Central
Shifnal
Landywood
Albrighton
Bloxwich North
Telford Steam Railway
Ironbridge
Cosford
Codsall
Codsall

1. Wigan North Western
2. Pemberton
3. Westhoughton
4. Farnworth
5. Moses Gate
6. Daisy Hill
7. Appley Bridge
8. Hall i' th' Wood
9. Bury South
10. Castleton
11. Rochdale
12. Newbold
13. Kingsway Business Park
14. Smithy Bridge
15. Warrington Central
16. Altrincham
17. Horwich Parkway
18. Manchester Airport

19B2

19B1

26A3   26B3

20

M 15 10 5 0 5 10 15 20 km

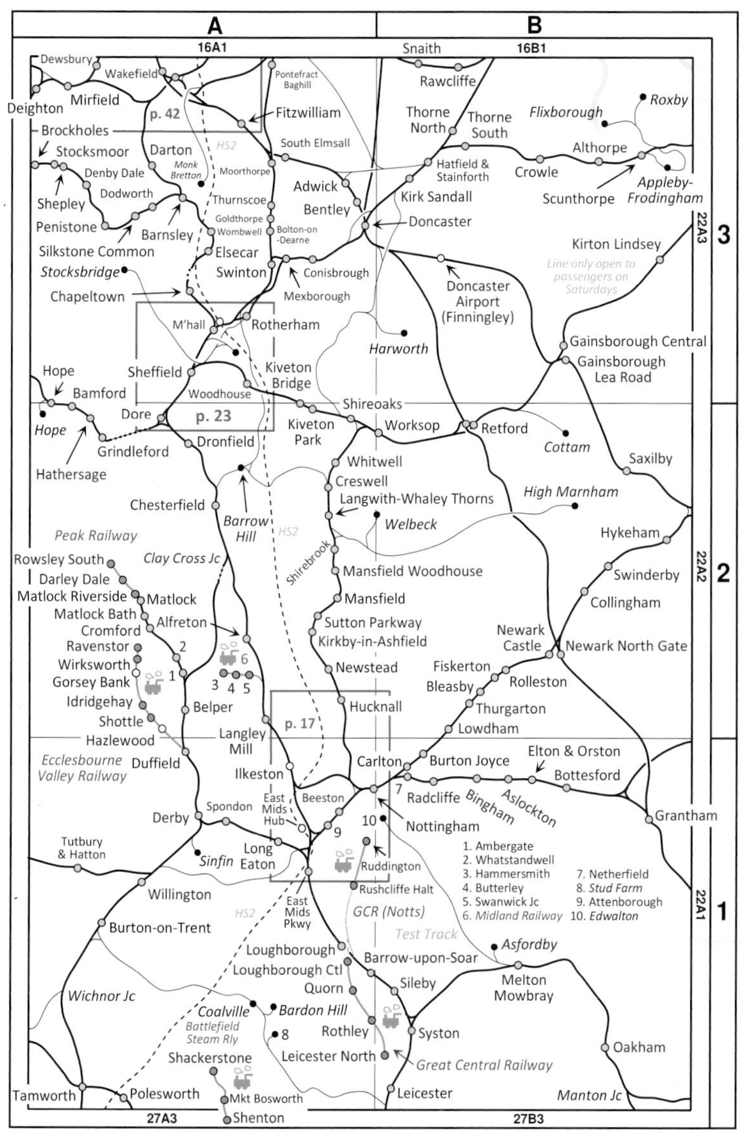

Snaith

Dewsbury
Wakefield
Deighton
Mirfield
Pontefract Baghill
Rawcliffe
Brockholes
Fitzwilliam
Thorne North
Thorne South
Flixborough
Roxby
Stocksmoor
Darton
p. 42
South Elmsall
Hatfield & Stainforth
Crowle
Althorpe
Scunthorpe
Appleby-Frodingham
Denby Dale
HS2
Monk Bretton
Moorthorpe
Shepley
Dodworth
Thurnscoe
Adwick
Kirk Sandall
Penistone
Barnsley
Goldthorpe
Wombwell
Bentley
Doncaster
Silkstone Common
Elsecar
Bolton-on-Dearne
Kirton Lindsey
Stocksbridge
Swinton
Conisbrough
Line only open to passengers on Saturdays
Chapeltown
M'hall
Rotherham
Mexborough
Doncaster Airport (Finningley)
Gainsborough Central
Hope
Bamford
Harworth
Gainsborough Lea Road
Sheffield
Kiveton Bridge
Dore
Woodhouse
p. 23
Shireoaks
Worksop
Retford
Hope
Grindleford
Dronfield
Kiveton Park
Cottam
Hathersage
Whitwell
Creswell
Saxilby
Chesterfield
Barrow Hill
Langwith-Whaley Thorns
Welbeck
High Marnham
Peak Railway
Clay Cross Jc
HS2
Shirebrook
Mansfield Woodhouse
Hykeham
Rowsley South
Darley Dale
Mansfield
Swinderby
Matlock
Collingham
Matlock Riverside
Alfreton
Sutton Parkway
Kirkby-in-Ashfield
Newark Castle
Newark North Gate
Matlock Bath
Cromford
2
6
Ravenstor
Wirksworth
1
3 4 5
Newstead
Fiskerton
Bleasby
Rolleston
Gorsey Bank
Idridgehay
Belper
Hucknall
Thurgarton
Shottle
Lowdham
Hazlewood
Ecclesbourne Valley Railway
Langley Mill
p. 17
Carlton
Burton Joyce
Elton & Orston
Duffield
Ilkeston
Beeston
Radcliffe
Bottesford
Spondon
East Mids Hub
7
Bingham
Aslockton
Derby
9
10
Grantham
Sinfin
Long Eaton
Nottingham
Tutbury & Hatton
Ruddington
1. Ambergate
Willington
Rushcliffe Halt
2. Whatstandwell
7. Netherfield
HS2
East Mids Pkwy
GCR (Notts)
3. Hammersmith
8. Stud Farm
Burton-on-Trent
Test Track
4. Butterley
9. Attenborough
5. Swanwick Jc
10. Edwalton
Wichnor Jc
Loughborough
Asfordby
6. *Midland Railway*
Loughborough Ctl
Barrow-upon-Soar
Coalville
Quorn
Sileby
Melton Mowbray
Bardon Hill
Battlefield Steam Rly
8
Rothley
Syston
Shackerstone
Leicester North
Great Central Railway
Oakham
Tamworth
Polesworth
Mkt Bosworth
Shenton
Leicester
Manton Jc

22A3
22A2
22A1
3
2
1

M 15   10   5   0   5   10   15   20 km

21

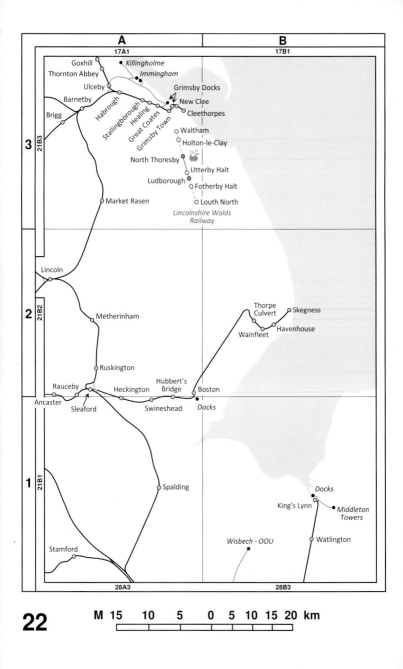

Goxhill
Thornton Abbey
● *Killingholme*
● *Immingham*
Ulceby
Barnetby
Grimsby Docks
New Clee
Brigg
Habrough
Stallingborough
Healing
Great Coates
Cleethorpes
Grimsby Town
○ Waltham
○ Holton-le-Clay

3

21B3

North Thoresby
○ Utterby Halt
Ludborough
○ Fotherby Halt
Market Rasen
○ Louth North
*Lincolnshire Wolds
Railway*

Lincoln

2

21B2

Metherinham
Thorpe
Culvert
Skegness
Wainfleet
Havenhouse

Ruskington
Raynceby
Heckington
Hubbert's
Bridge
Boston
Ancaster
Sleaford
Swineshead
Docks

1

21B1

Spalding
Docks
King's Lynn
● *Middleton
Towers*
Wisbech - OOU
○ Watlington

Stamford

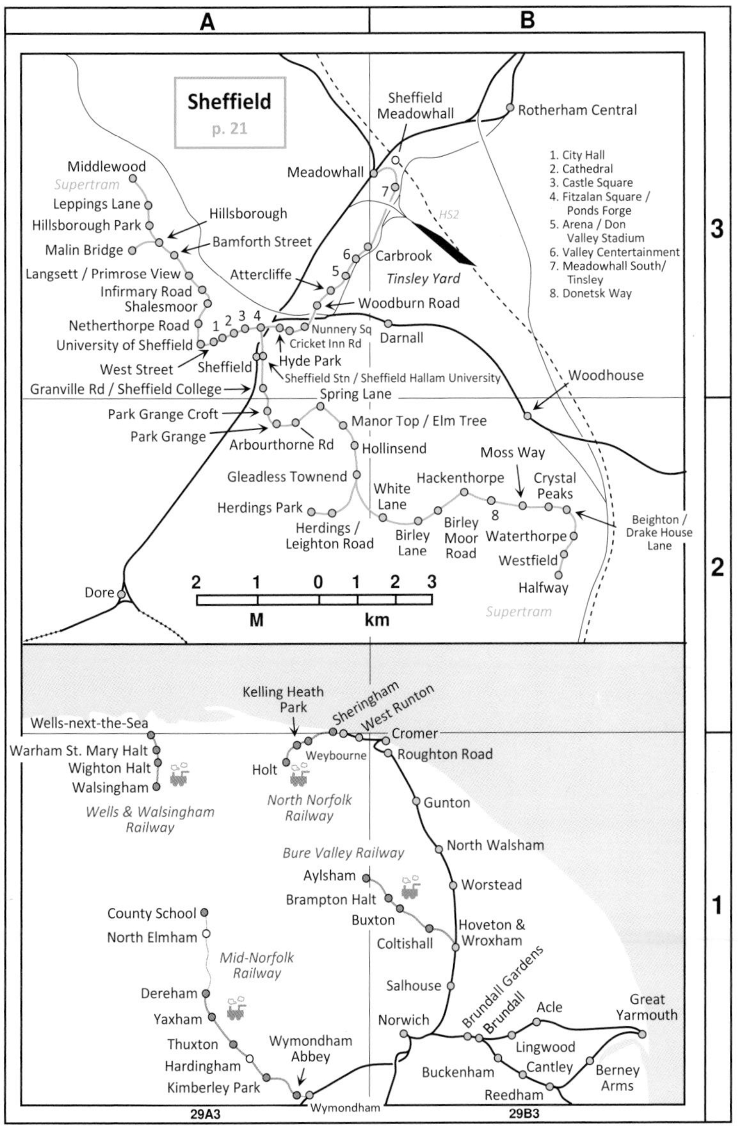

Sheffield
p. 21

Supertram

Middlewood
Leppings Lane
Hillsborough Park
Hillsborough
Malin Bridge
Bamforth Street
Langsett / Primrose View
Infirmary Road
Attercliffe
Shalesmoor
Netherthorpe Road
University of Sheffield
West Street
Sheffield
Granville Rd / Sheffield College
Park Grange Croft
Park Grange
Arbourthorne Rd
Gleadless Townend
Herdings Park
Herdings / Leighton Road

Sheffield Meadowhall
Rotherham Central
Meadowhall

1. City Hall
2. Cathedral
3. Castle Square
4. Fitzalan Square / Ponds Forge
5. Arena / Don Valley Stadium
6. Valley Centertainment
7. Meadowhall South / Tinsley
8. Donetsk Way

HS2

7

Carbrook
6
5
Tinsley Yard
Woodburn Road
Nunnery Sq
1 2 3 4
Cricket Inn Rd
Darnall
Hyde Park
Sheffield Stn / Sheffield Hallam University
Woodhouse
Spring Lane
Manor Top / Elm Tree
Hollinsend
Hackenthorpe
Moss Way
Crystal Peaks
White Lane
Birley Moor Road
8
Waterthorpe
Beighton / Drake House Lane
Birley Lane
Westfield
Halfway
Supertram
Dore

2 1 0 1 2 3
M   km

Wells-next-the-Sea
Kelling Heath Park
Sheringham
West Runton
Warham St. Mary Halt
Wighton Halt
Walsingham
Wells & Walsingham Railway
Holt
Weybourne
Cromer
Roughton Road
North Norfolk Railway
Gunton
North Walsham
Bure Valley Railway
Aylsham
Worstead
Brampton Halt
Buxton
Hoveton & Wroxham
County School
North Elmham
Coltishall
Mid-Norfolk Railway
Salhouse
Brundall Gardens
Acle
Great Yarmouth
Dereham
Yaxham
Norwich
Brundall
Lingwood
Thuxton
Cantley
Hardingham
Wymondham Abbey
Buckenham
Berney Arms
Kimberley Park
Reedham
Wymondham

29A3

29B3

M 15   10   5   0   5   10   15   20 km

23

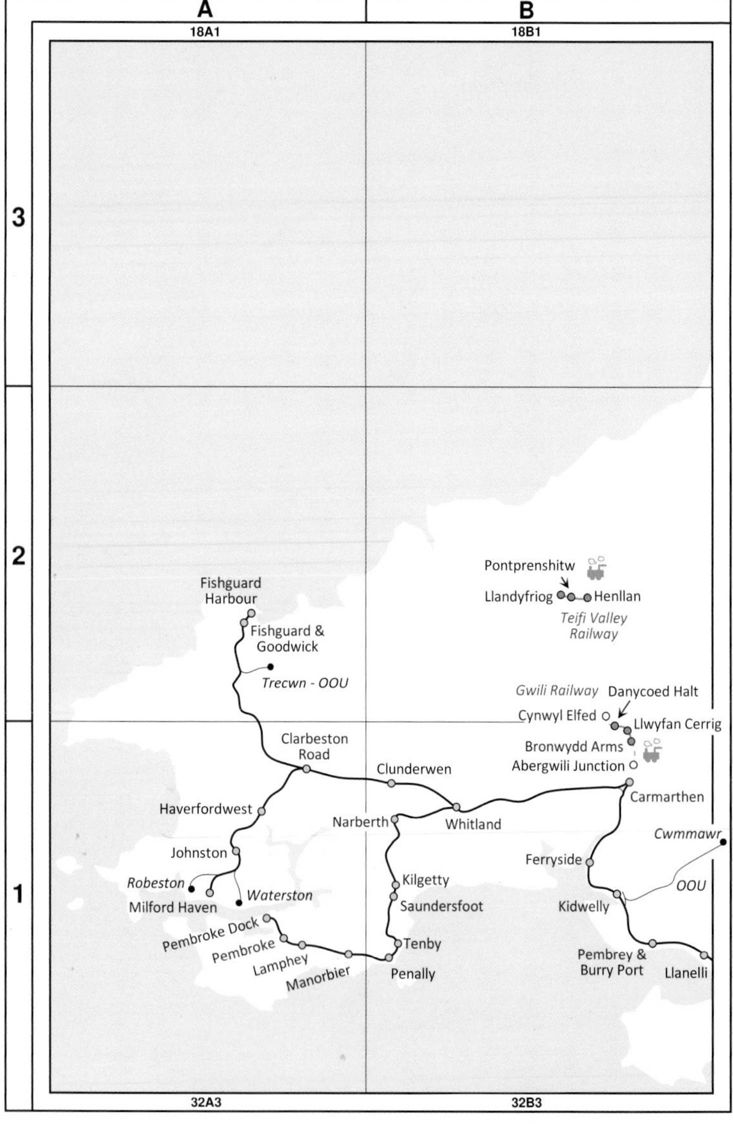

3

2

Fishguard
Harbour

Fishguard &
Goodwick

Trecwn - OOU

Pontprenshitw

Llandyfriog ●○● Henllan

*Teifi Valley
Railway*

Gwili Railway Danycoed Halt
Cynwyl Elfed ○↙
Llwyfan Cerrig

Clarbeston
Road

Clunderwen

Bronwydd Arms
Abergwili Junction

Carmarthen

Haverfordwest

Narberth   Whitland

Cwmmawr

Johnston

Ferryside

Robeston   *Waterston*

Milford Haven

Kilgetty

OOU

Pembroke Dock

Saundersfoot

Kidwelly

1

Pembroke

Tenby

Lamphey

Penally

Pembrey &
Burry Port   Llanelli

Manorbier

M 15   10   5   0   5   10 15 20 km

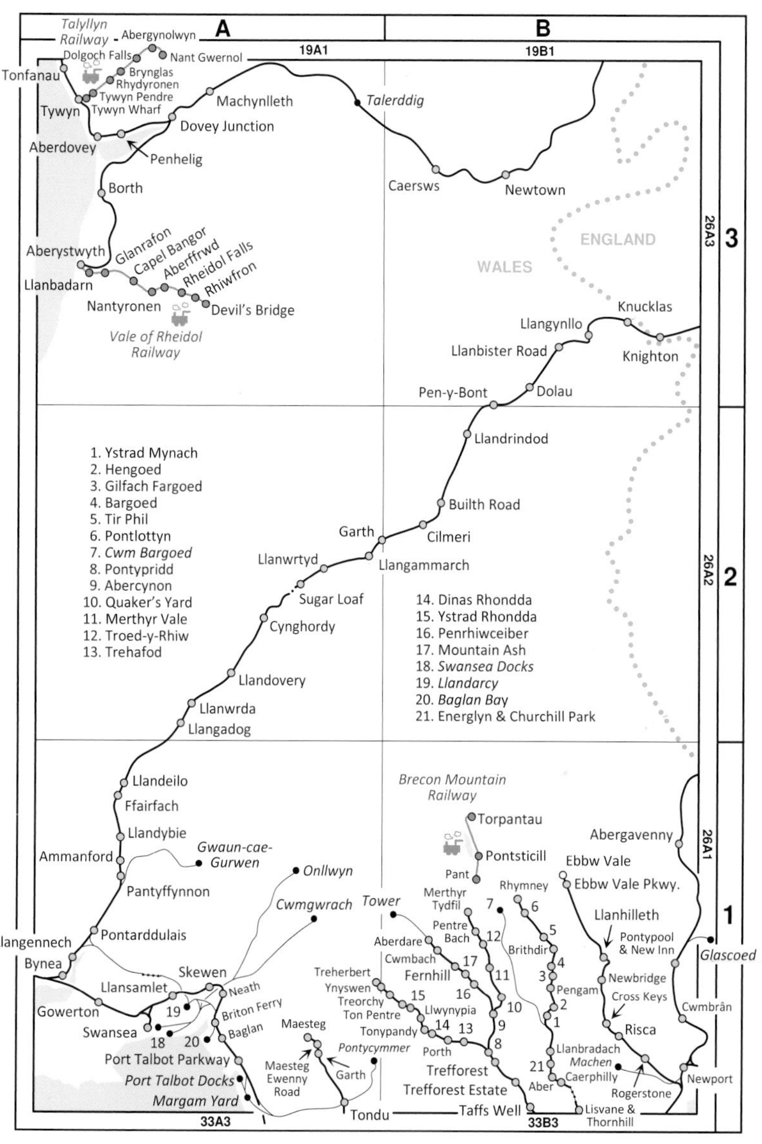

Talyllyn Railway
Abergynolwyn
Nant Gwernol
Dolgoch Falls
Tonfanau
Brynglas
Rhydyronen
Tywyn Pendre
Tywyn
Tywyn Wharf
Aberdovey
Penhelig
Borth

Machynlleth
Dovey Junction
Talerddig

Caersws
Newton

ENGLAND
WALES

Aberystwyth
Glanrafon
Capel Bangor
Aberffrwd
Rheidol Falls
Llanbadarn
Nantyronen
Rhiwfron
Devil's Bridge
Vale of Rheidol Railway

Knucklas
Llangynllo
Knighton
Llanbister Road
Pen-y-Bont
Dolau
Llandrindod

1. Ystrad Mynach
2. Hengoed
3. Gilfach Fargoed
4. Bargoed
5. Tir Phil
6. Pontlottyn
7. Cwm Bargoed
8. Pontypridd
9. Abercynon
10. Quaker's Yard
11. Merthyr Vale
12. Troed-y-Rhiw
13. Trehafod

Builth Road
Garth
Cilmeri
Llanwrtyd
Llangammarch
Sugar Loaf
Cynghordy

14. Dinas Rhondda
15. Ystrad Rhondda
16. Penrhiwceiber
17. Mountain Ash
18. Swansea Docks
19. Llandarcy
20. Baglan Bay
21. Energlyn & Churchill Park

Llandovery
Llanwrda
Llangadog

Llandeilo
Ffairfach
Llandybie
Ammanford
Pantyffynnon
Gwaun-cae-Gurwen
Onllwyn
Cwmgwrach
Tower
Brecon Mountain Railway
Torpantau
Pontsticill
Pant
Rhymney
Abergavenny
Ebbw Vale
Ebbw Vale Pkwy.
Merthyr Tydfil
Llanhilleth
Pentre Bach
Pontypool & New Inn
Aberdare
Glascoed
Cwmbach
Fernhill
Brithdir
Newbridge
Cross Keys
Pengam
Cwmbrân
Langennech
Bynea
Pontarddulais
Skewen
Neath
Llansamlet
Briton Ferry
Baglan
Gowerton
Swansea
Port Talbot Parkway
Port Talbot Docks
Margam Yard
Maesteg
Maesteg Ewenny Road
Garth
Tondu
Treherbert
Ynyswen
Treorchy
Ton Pentre
Tonypandy
Pontycymmer
Porth
Trefforest
Trefforest Estate
Taffs Well
Llwynypia
Trefforest
Aber
Risca
Llanbradach
Machen
Caerphilly
Rogerstone
Newport
Lisvane & Thornhill

M 15 10 5 0 5 10 15 20 km

25

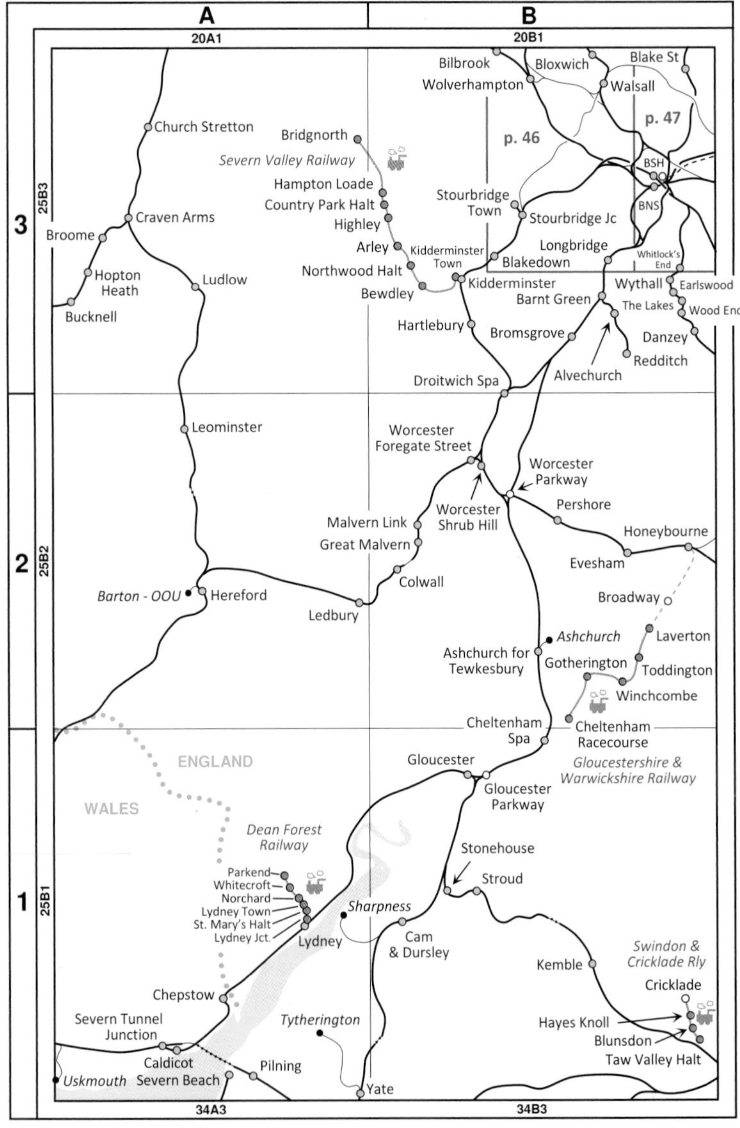

Bilbrook
Bloxwich
Blake St
Wolverhampton
Walsall

p. 47

p. 46

Church Stretton
Bridgnorth
Severn Valley Railway
Hampton Loade
Country Park Halt
Highley
Stourbridge Town
BSH
Stourbridge Jc
BNS
Craven Arms
Broome
Arley
Kidderminster Town
Longbridge
Blakedown
Whitlock's End
Hopton Heath
Ludlow
Northwood Halt
Kidderminster
Wythall
Earlswood
Bewdley
Barnt Green
The Lakes
Wood End
Bucknell
Hartlebury
Bromsgrove
Danzey
Alvechurch
Redditch
Droitwich Spa

Leominster

Worcester Foregate Street
Worcester Parkway
Pershore
Honeybourne
Malvern Link
Great Malvern
Worcester Shrub Hill
Evesham
Broadway
Barton - OOU
Hereford
Colwall
Laverton
Ledbury
Ashchurch
Ashchurch for Tewkesbury
Gotherington
Toddington
Winchcombe
Cheltenham Spa
Cheltenham Racecourse

Gloucestershire & Warwickshire Railway

ENGLAND

Gloucester

WALES

Gloucester Parkway
Stonehouse
Dean Forest Railway
Stroud
Parkend
Whitecroft
Norchard
Lydney Town
St. Mary's Halt
Lydney Jct.
Sharpness
Lydney
Cam & Dursley
Swindon & Cricklade Rly
Kemble
Cricklade
Chepstow
Tytherington
Hayes Knoll
Severn Tunnel Junction
Blunsdon
Taw Valley Halt
Uskmouth
Caldicot
Severn Beach
Pilning
Yate

M 15 10 5 0 5 10 15 20 km

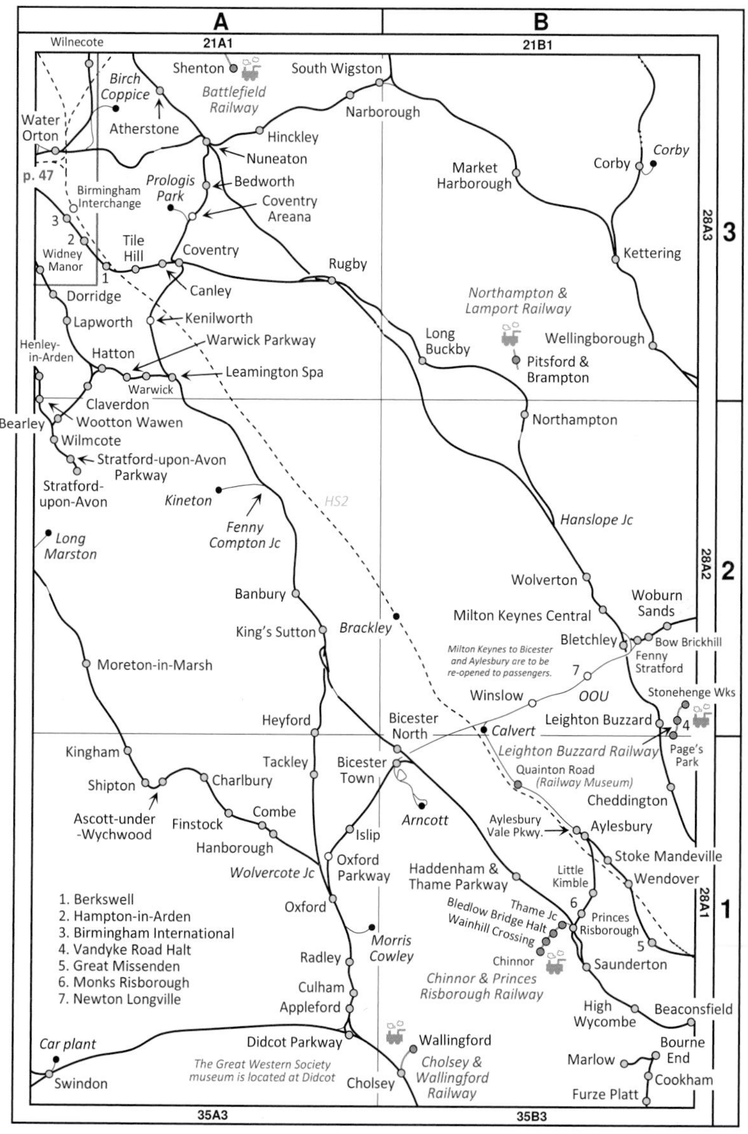

A | B

Wilnecote

Shenton

South Wigston

Birch
Coppice

Battlefield
Railway

Water
Orton

Atherstone

Hinckley

Narborough

p. 47

Nuneaton

Market
Harborough

Corby

Corby

Birmingham
Interchange

Prologis
Park

Bedworth

3

Coventry
Areana

Kettering

2

Widney
Manor

1

Tile
Hill

Coventry

Rugby

28A3

3

Dorridge

Canley

Lapworth

Kenilworth

Northampton &
Lamport Railway

Henley-
in-Arden

Hatton

Warwick Parkway

Long
Buckby

Wellingborough

Leamington Spa

Pitsford &
Brampton

Bearley

Claverdon

Warwick

Wootton Wawen

Wilmcote

Northampton

Stratford-upon-Avon
Parkway

Stratford-
upon-Avon

Kineton

Hanslope Jc

28A2

2

Long
Marston

Fenny
Compton Jc

HS2

Wolverton

Woburn
Sands

Banbury

Brackley

Milton Keynes Central

Bow Brickhill

King's Sutton

*Milton Keynes to Bicester
and Aylesbury are to be
re-opened to passengers.*

Bletchley

Fenny
Stratford

Moreton-in-Marsh

7

Winslow

OOU

Stonehenge Wks

Heyford

Bicester
North

Calvert

Leighton Buzzard

4

Kingham

Tackley

Bicester
Town

Leighton Buzzard Railway

Page's
Park

Shipton

Charlbury

Combe

Quainton Road
(Railway Museum)

Cheddington

Ascott-under
-Wychwood

Finstock

Arncott

Aylesbury
Vale Pkwy.

Aylesbury

Hanborough

Islip

Haddenham &
Thame Parkway

Little
Kimble

Stoke Mandeville

Wendover

Wolvercote Jc

Oxford
Parkway

Thame Jc

6

Princes
Risborough

Oxford

Bledlow Bridge Halt
Wainhill Crossing

5

1. Berkswell
2. Hampton-in-Arden
3. Birmingham International
4. Vandyke Road Halt
5. Great Missenden
6. Monks Risborough
7. Newton Longville

Morris
Cowley

Radley

Chinnor

Saunderton

*Chinnor & Princes
Risborough Railway*

Culham

High
Wycombe

Beaconsfield

Appleford

Bourne
End

Car plant

Didcot Parkway

Wallingford

Marlow

Cookham

Swindon

*The Great Western Society
museum is located at Didcot*

*Cholsey &
Wallingford
Railway*

Cholsey

Furze Platt

28A1

1

M 15 10 5 0 5 10 15 20 km

27

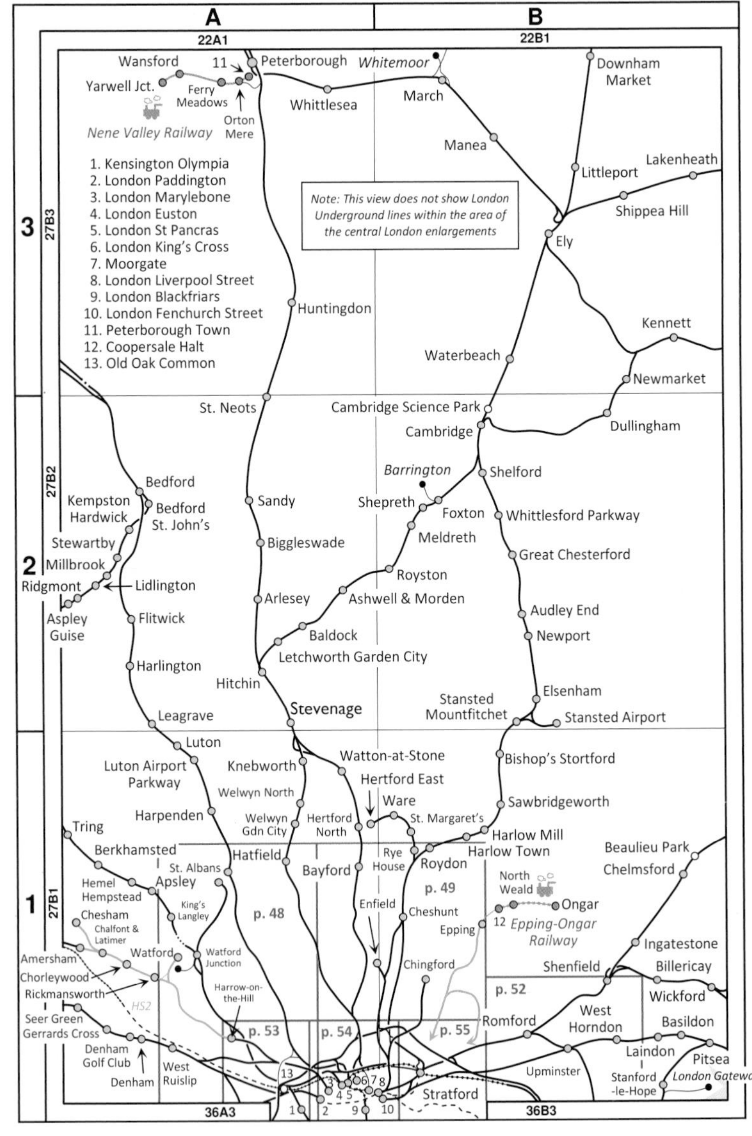

A

22A1

Wansford
11
Peterborough
Whitemoor
Yarwell Jct.
Ferry Meadows
Whittlesea
March
Orton Mere

Nene Valley Railway

1. Kensington Olympia
2. London Paddington
3. London Marylebone
4. London Euston
5. London St Pancras
6. London King's Cross
7. Moorgate
8. London Liverpool Street
9. London Blackfriars
10. London Fenchurch Street
11. Peterborough Town
12. Coopersale Halt
13. Old Oak Common

Note: This view does not show London Underground lines within the area of the central London enlargements

Huntingdon

St. Neots

Cambridge Science Park

Cambridge

Barrington

Bedford
Kempston Hardwick
Bedford St. John's
Sandy
Shepreth
Foxton
Whittlesford Parkway
Stewartby
Shelford
Millbrook
Biggleswade
Meldreth
Great Chesterford
Ridgmont
Lidlington
Royston
Aspley Guise
Flitwick
Arlesey
Ashwell & Morden
Audley End
Harlington
Baldock
Newport
Letchworth Garden City
Hitchin
Leagrave
Stevenage
Elsenham
Stansted Mountfitchet
Stansted Airport
Luton

Luton Airport Parkway
Knebworth
Watton-at-Stone
Bishop's Stortford
Welwyn North
Hertford East
Tring
Harpenden
Welwyn Gdn City
Hertford North
Ware
St. Margaret's
Sawbridgeworth
Berkhamsted
Hatfield
Rye House
Roydon
Harlow Mill
Beaulieu Park
Hemel Hempstead
Apsley
Bayford
p. 49
North Weald
Harlow Town
Chelmsford
Chesham
King's Langley
Enfield
Cheshunt
Ongar
Chalfont & Latimer
Watford
Epping
12 *Epping-Ongar Railway*
Amersham
Watford Junction
Chingford
Ingatestone
Chorleywood
Harrow-on-the-Hill
Shenfield
Billericay
Rickmansworth
HS2
p. 53
p. 54
p. 52
Romford
West Horndon
Wickford
Seer Green
Gerrards Cross
p. 55
Basildon
Denham Golf Club
Upminster
Laindon
Pitsea
West Ruislip
13
Stanford-le-Hope
London Gateway
Denham
Stratford

B

22B1

Downham Market
Lakenheath
Littleport
Shippea Hill
Manea
Ely
Kennett
Waterbeach
Newmarket
Dullingham

28

M 15   10   5   0   5   10   15   20 km

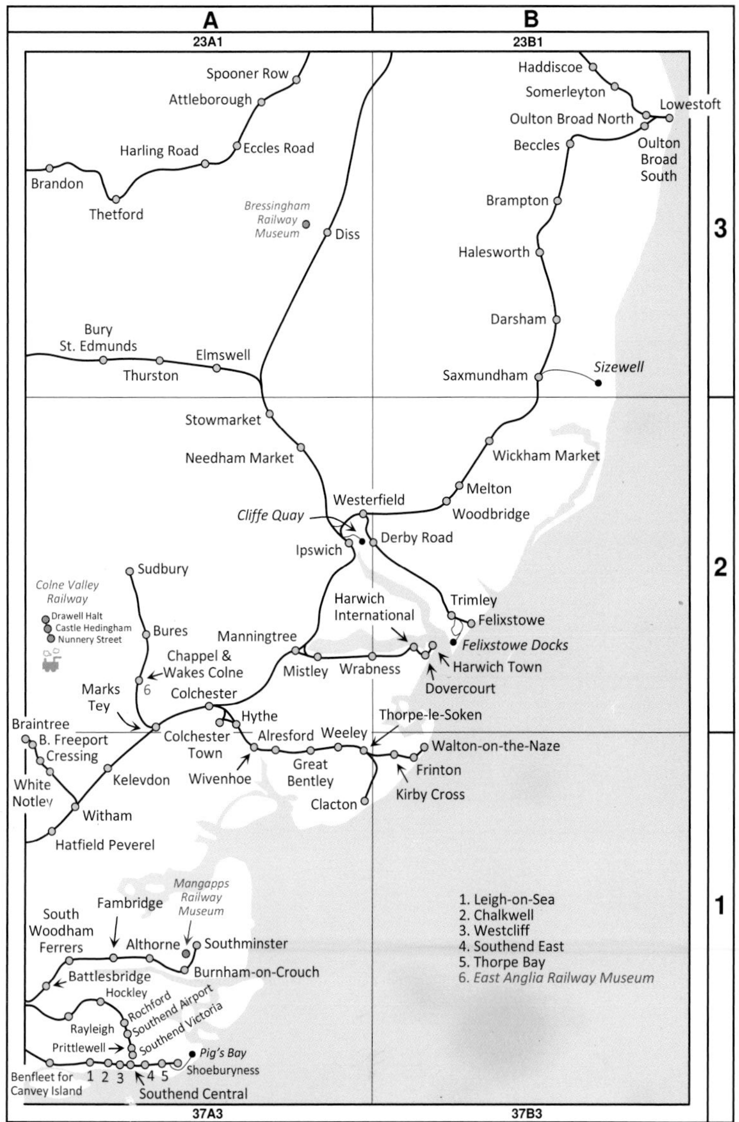

3

Spooner Row
Haddiscoe
Somerleyton
Attleborough
Oulton Broad North
Lowestoft
Harling Road
Eccles Road
Beccles
Oulton Broad South
Brandon
Thetford
Brampton
Bressingham Railway Museum
Diss
Halesworth
Bury St. Edmunds
Darsham
Elmswell
Thurston
Saxmundham
Sizewell

2

Stowmarket
Wickham Market
Needham Market
Westerfield
Melton
Cliffe Quay
Woodbridge
Ipswich
Derby Road
Colne Valley Railway
Sudbury
Trimley
Felixstowe
Drawell Halt
Castle Hedingham
Nunnery Street
Bures
Harwich International
Felixstowe Docks
Manningtree
Chappel & Wakes Colne
Mistley
Wrabness
Harwich Town
Marks Tey
6
Colchester
Dovercourt
Braintree
Hythe
Thorpe-le-Soken
B. Freeport Crossing
Colchester Town
Alresford
Weeley
Walton-on-the-Naze
White Notley
Kelvedon
Wivenhoe
Great Bentley
Frinton
Witham
Clacton
Kirby Cross
Hatfield Peverel

1

Mangapps Railway Museum
South Woodham Ferrers
Fambridge
Althorne
Southminster
Battlesbridge
Burnham-on-Crouch
Hockley
Rochford
Rayleigh
Southend Airport
Prittlewell
Southend Victoria
Benfleet for Canvey Island
1 2 3 4 5
Pig's Bay
Shoeburyness
Southend Central

1. Leigh-on-Sea
2. Chalkwell
3. Westcliff
4. Southend East
5. Thorpe Bay
6. *East Anglia Railway Museum*

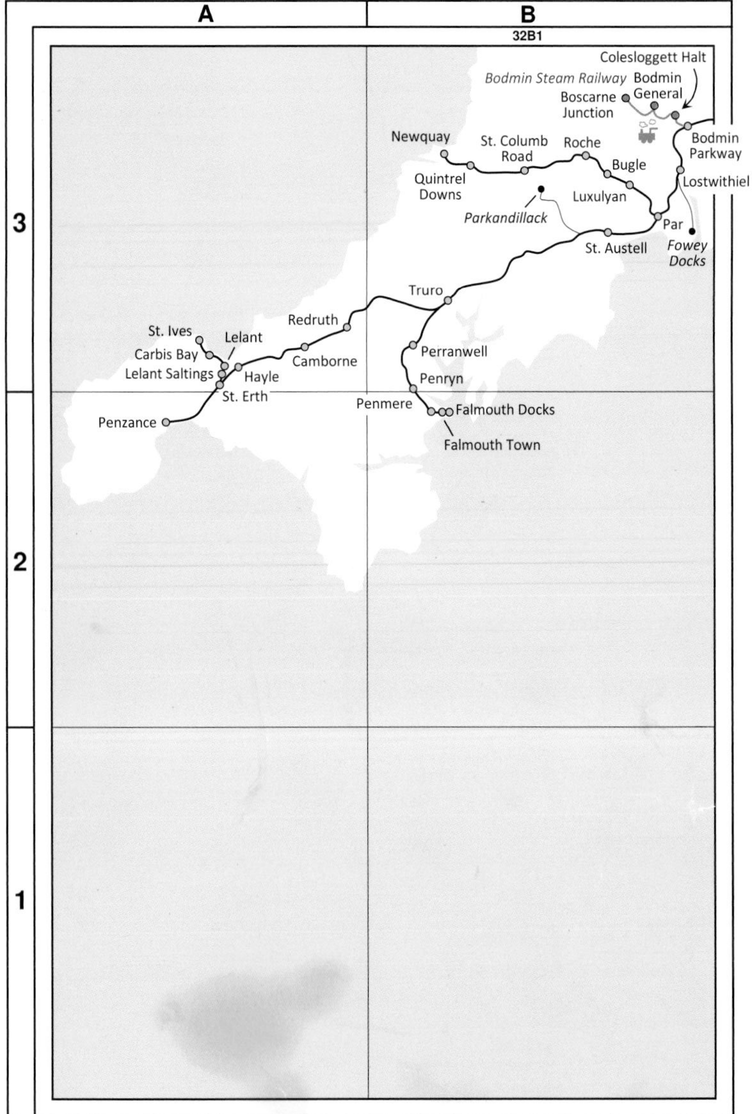

32B1

Colesloggett Halt
Bodmin Steam Railway Bodmin
Boscarne General
Junction
Bodmin
Parkway

Newquay St. Columb Roche
   Road   Bugle Lostwithiel
Quintrel   Luxulyan
Downs *Parkandillack*   Par
      St. Austell *Fowey
         Docks*

    Truro
  Redruth
St. Ives Lelant
Carbis Bay Camborne Perranwell
Lelant Saltings Hayle Penryn
  St. Erth Penmere
Penzance   Falmouth Docks
       Falmouth Town

3

2

1

30 M 15 10 5 0 5 10 15 20 km

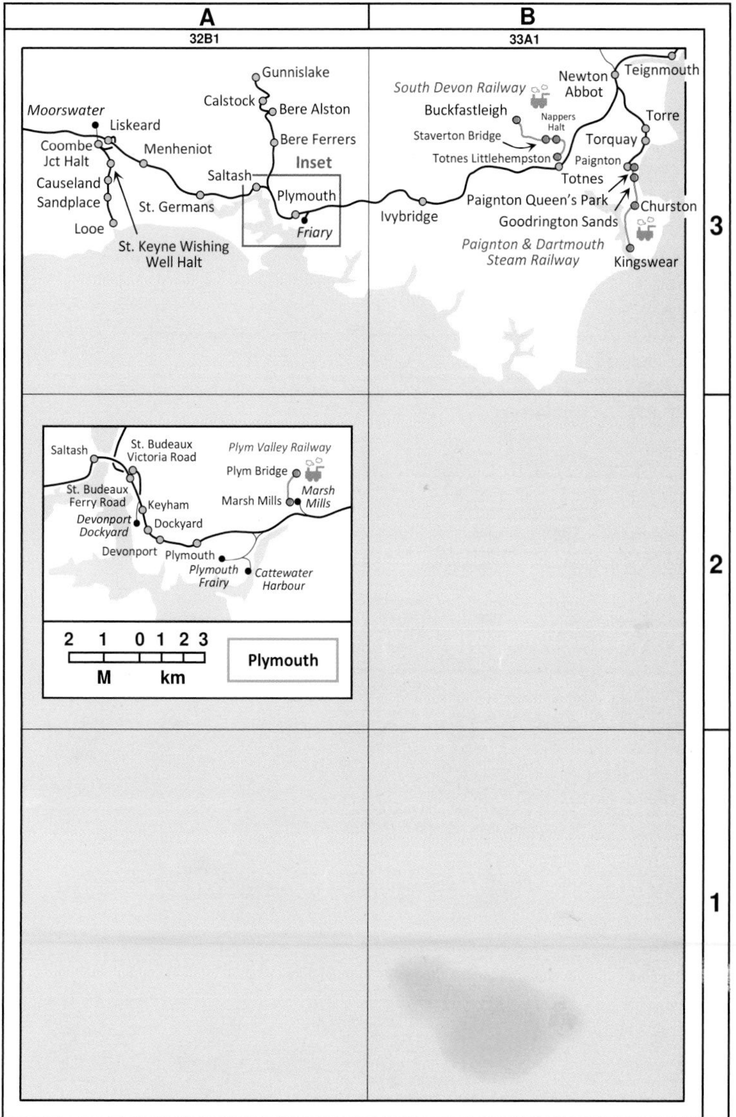

	A	B	
	32B1	33A1	

Moorswater
Gunnislake
Calstock
Bere Alston
Coombe Jct Halt
Liskeard
Menheniot
Bere Ferrers
Causeland
Sandplace
Saltash
Inset
St. Germans
Plymouth
Looe
St. Keyne Wishing Well Halt
Friary

South Devon Railway
Newton Abbot
Teignmouth
Buckfastleigh
Nappers Halt
Torre
Staverton Bridge
Torquay
Totnes Littlehempston
Paignton
Totnes
Ivybridge
Paignton Queen's Park
Goodrington Sands
Churston
Paignton & Dartmouth Steam Railway
Kingswear

Inset (Plymouth):

Saltash
St. Budeaux Victoria Road
Plym Valley Railway
Plym Bridge
St. Budeaux Ferry Road
Keyham
Devonport Dockyard
Dockyard
Marsh Mills
Marsh Mills
Devonport
Plymouth
Plymouth *Friary*
Cattewater Harbour

2 1 0 1 2 3
M   km

Plymouth

3

2

1

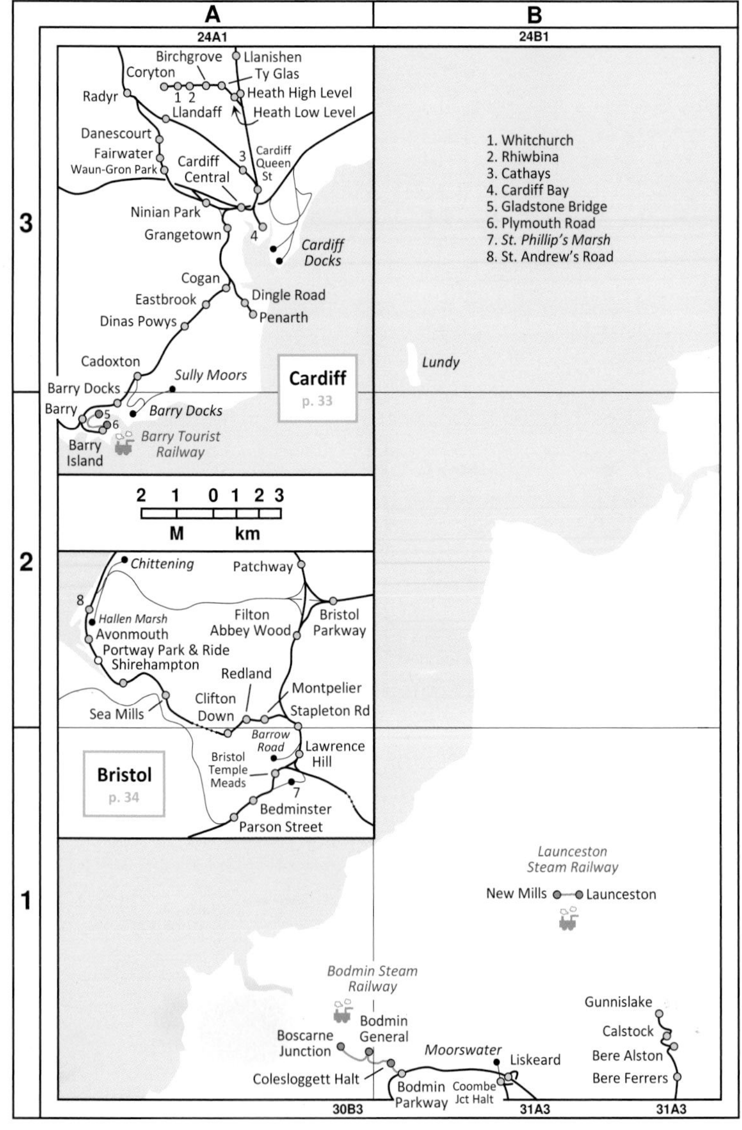

	A	B
	24A1	24B1

Birchgrove
Coryton
Llanishen
Ty Glas
Radyr
Heath High Level
1 2
Llandaff
Heath Low Level
Danescourt
Fairwater
3
Cardiff
Waun-Gron Park
Queen St
Cardiff Central
Ninian Park
Grangetown
Cardiff
4
Docks
Cogan
Eastbrook
Dingle Road
Dinas Powys
Penarth
Cadoxton
Barry Docks
Sully Moors
Barry
Barry Docks
5
6
Barry Island
Barry Tourist
Railway

1. Whitchurch
2. Rhiwbina
3. Cathays
4. Cardiff Bay
5. Gladstone Bridge
6. Plymouth Road
7. St. Phillip's Marsh
8. St. Andrew's Road

Cardiff
p. 33

Lundy

2 1 0 1 2 3
M   km

Chittening
Patchway
8
Hallen Marsh
Filton
Avonmouth
Abbey Wood
Bristol
Portway Park & Ride
Parkway
Shirehampton
Redland
Sea Mills
Clifton
Down
Montpelier
Stapleton Rd
Barrow
Road
Lawrence
Hill
Bristol
p. 34
Bristol Temple
Meads
7
Bedminster
Parson Street

Launceston
Steam Railway
New Mills Launceston

Bodmin Steam
Railway
Gunnislake
Calstock
Boscarne
Junction
Bodmin
General
Moorswater
Liskeard
Bere Alston
Colesloggett Halt
Bodmin
Parkway
Coombe
Jct Halt
Bere Ferrers

30B3	31A3	31A3

32   M 15 10 5 0 5 10 15 20 km

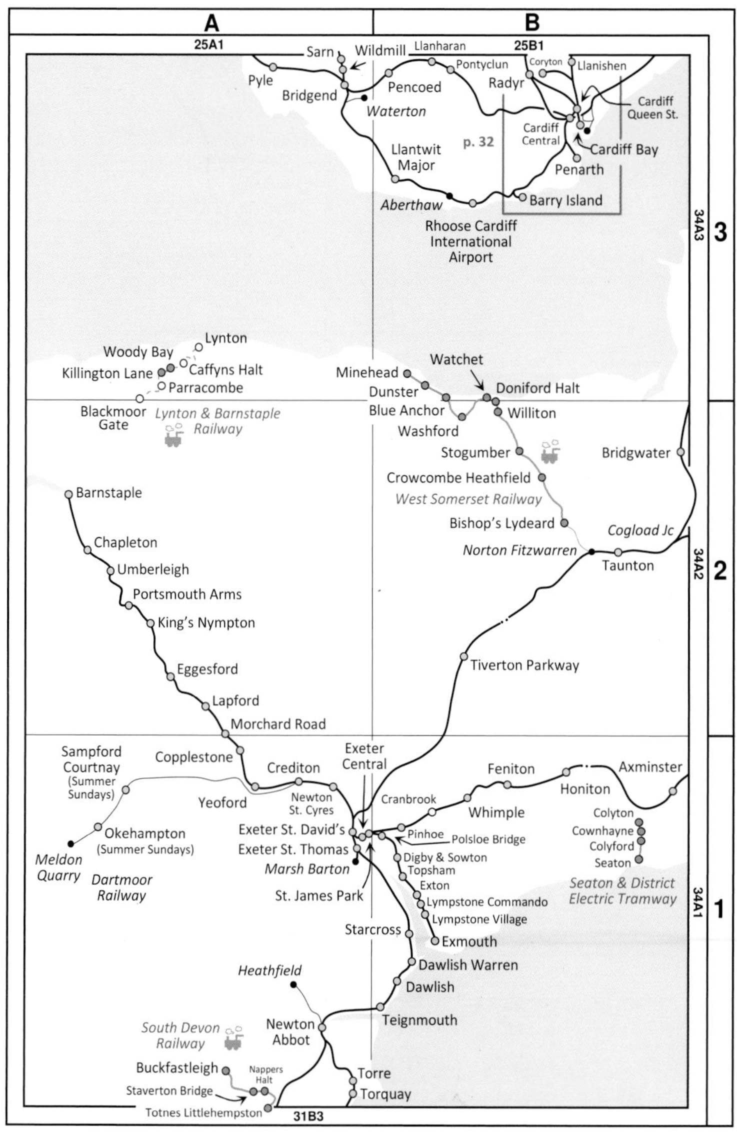

25A1   25B1

Sarn   Wildmill   Llanharan
Pyle   Pontyclun   Coryton   Llanishen
Bridgend   Pencoed   Radyr
Waterton   Cardiff Queen St.
Cardiff Central
Llantwit Major   p. 32   Cardiff Bay
Penarth
Aberthaw   Barry Island
Rhoose Cardiff International Airport

34A3   **3**

Lynton
Woody Bay
Killington Lane   Caffyns Halt
Parracombe
Blackmoor Gate   *Lynton & Barnstaple Railway*
Watchet
Minehead   Doniford Halt
Dunster
Blue Anchor   Williton
Washford
Stogumber   Bridgwater
Barnstaple   Crowcombe Heathfield
West Somerset Railway
Chapleton   Bishop's Lydeard
Umberleigh   *Norton Fitzwarren*   *Cogload Jc*
Portsmouth Arms   Taunton
King's Nympton
Eggesford
Lapford   Tiverton Parkway
Morchard Road

34A2   **2**

Sampford Courtenay (Summer Sundays)
Copplestone   Exeter Central
Crediton   Feniton   Axminster
Yeoford   Newton St. Cyres   Cranbrook   Honiton
Okehampton (Summer Sundays)   Whimple   Colyton
Meldon Quarry   Pinhoe   Polsloe Bridge   Cownhayne
Dartmoor Railway   Exeter St. David's   Colyford
Exeter St. Thomas   Digby & Sowton   Seaton
Marsh Barton   Topsham   *Seaton & District Electric Tramway*
St. James Park   Exton
Lympstone Commando
Lympstone Village
Starcross   Exmouth
Heathfield   Dawlish Warren
Dawlish
South Devon Railway   Newton Abbot   Teignmouth
Buckfastleigh   Nappers Halt
Staverton Bridge   Torre
Totnes Littlehempston   Torquay

31B3

34A1   **1**

M 15   10   5   0   5   10   15   20 km

33

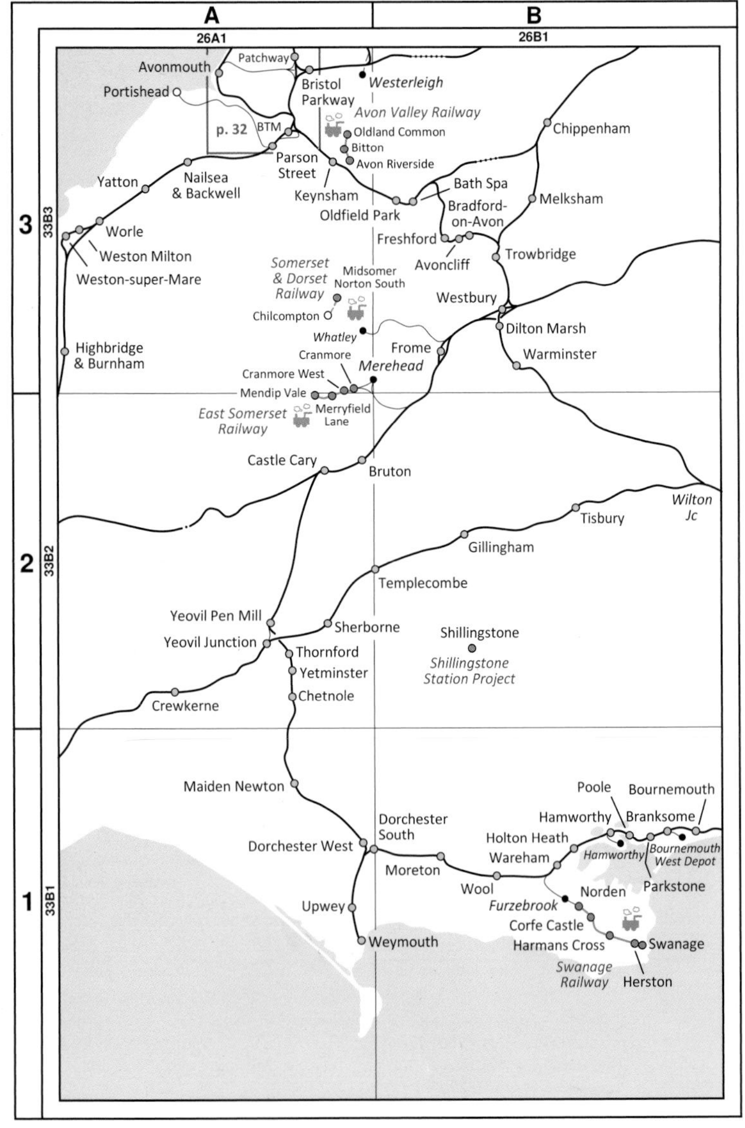

Avonmouth
Portishead ○   Patchway
Bristol
Parkway   *Westerleigh*
Avon Valley Railway   Chippenham
p. 32   BTM   Oldland Common
Parson   Bitton
Street   Avon Riverside
Yatton   Nailsea   Keynsham   Bath Spa
& Backwell   Oldfield Park   Bradford-
on-Avon   Melksham
Worle   Freshford
Weston Milton   Avoncliff   Trowbridge
Weston-super-Mare   *Somerset &   Midsomer   Westbury
Dorset   Norton South   Dilton Marsh
Railway*   Chilcompton ○   Warminster
Highbridge   *Whatley*   Frome
& Burnham   Cranmore
Cranmore West   *Merehead*
Mendip Vale
*East Somerset   Merryfield
Railway*   Lane
Castle Cary   Bruton
*Wilton
Jc*
Tisbury
Gillingham
Templecombe
Yeovil Pen Mill   Sherborne
Yeovil Junction   Shillingstone
Thornford   *Shillingstone
Yetminster   Station Project*
Crewkerne   Chetnole

Maiden Newton   Poole   Bournemouth
Dorchester   Hamworthy   Branksome
Holton Heath   *Hamworthy*   *Bournemouth
Dorchester West   Wareham   West Depot*
Moreton   Norden   Parkstone
Wool   *Furzebrook*
Upwey   Corfe Castle   Swanage
Harmans Cross
○ Weymouth   *Swanage   Herston
Railway*

34   M 15   10   5   0   5   10   15   20 km

33B3   33B2   33B1   (margin labels)

3

2

1

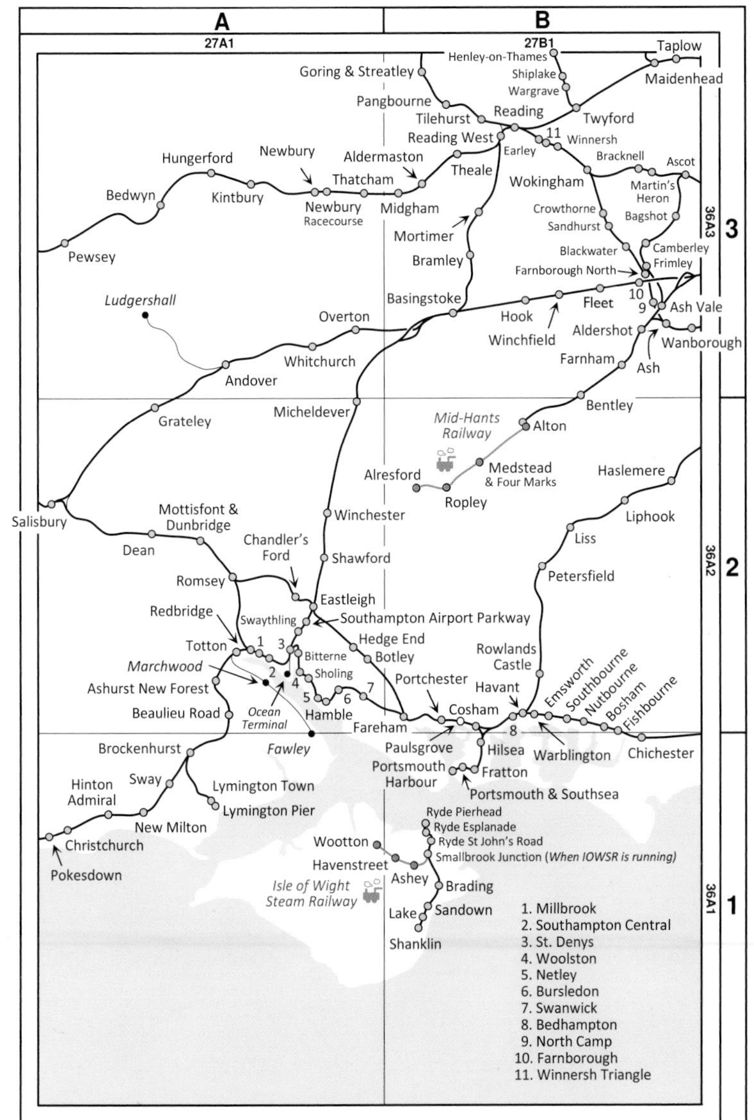

Taplow
Henley-on-Thames
Shiplake
Maidenhead
Goring & Streatley
Wargrave
Pangbourne
Tilehurst
Reading
Twyford
Reading West
11
Winnersh
Hungerford
Newbury
Aldermaston
Earley
Bracknell
Ascot
Bedwyn
Kintbury
Thatcham
Theale
Wokingham
Martin's
Heron
Newbury
Racecourse
Midgham
Crowthorne
Sandhurst
Bagshot
Pewsey
Mortimer
Blackwater
Camberley
Frimley
Bramley
Farnborough North
10
Ash Vale
Basingstoke
Hook
Fleet
9
Wanborough
Ludgershall
Overton
Winchfield
Aldershot
Whitchurch
Farnham
Ash
Andover
Micheldever
Bentley
Grateley
*Mid-Hants
Railway*
Alton
Haslemere
Alresford
Medstead
& Four Marks
Salisbury
Mottisfont &
Dunbridge
Winchester
Ropley
Liphook
Dean
Chandler's
Ford
Shawford
Liss
Romsey
Petersfield
Redbridge
Eastleigh
Swaythling
Southampton Airport Parkway
Totton
1
Hedge End
Rowlands
Castle
Emsworth
Southbourne
Nutbourne
Bosham
Fishbourne
Marchwood
3
Bitterne
Botley
2
Sholing
Portchester
Havant
Ashurst New Forest
4
7
Beaulieu Road
*Ocean
Terminal*
5
6
Hamble
Portslade
Cosham
8
Warblington
Chichester
Brockenhurst
Fawley
Fareham
Paulsgrove
Hilsea
Portsmouth
Harbour
Fratton
Hinton
Admiral
Sway
Lymington Town
Portsmouth & Southsea
New Milton
Lymington Pier
Christchurch
Wootton
Ryde Pierhead
Ryde Esplanade
Ryde St John's Road
Smallbrook Junction *(When IOWSR is running)*
Pokesdown
Havenstreet
Ashey
Brading
*Isle of Wight
Steam Railway*
Lake
Sandown
Shanklin

1. Millbrook
2. Southampton Central
3. St. Denys
4. Woolston
5. Netley
6. Bursledon
7. Swanwick
8. Bedhampton
9. North Camp
10. Farnborough
11. Winnersh Triangle

M 15   10   5   0   5   10   15 20 km

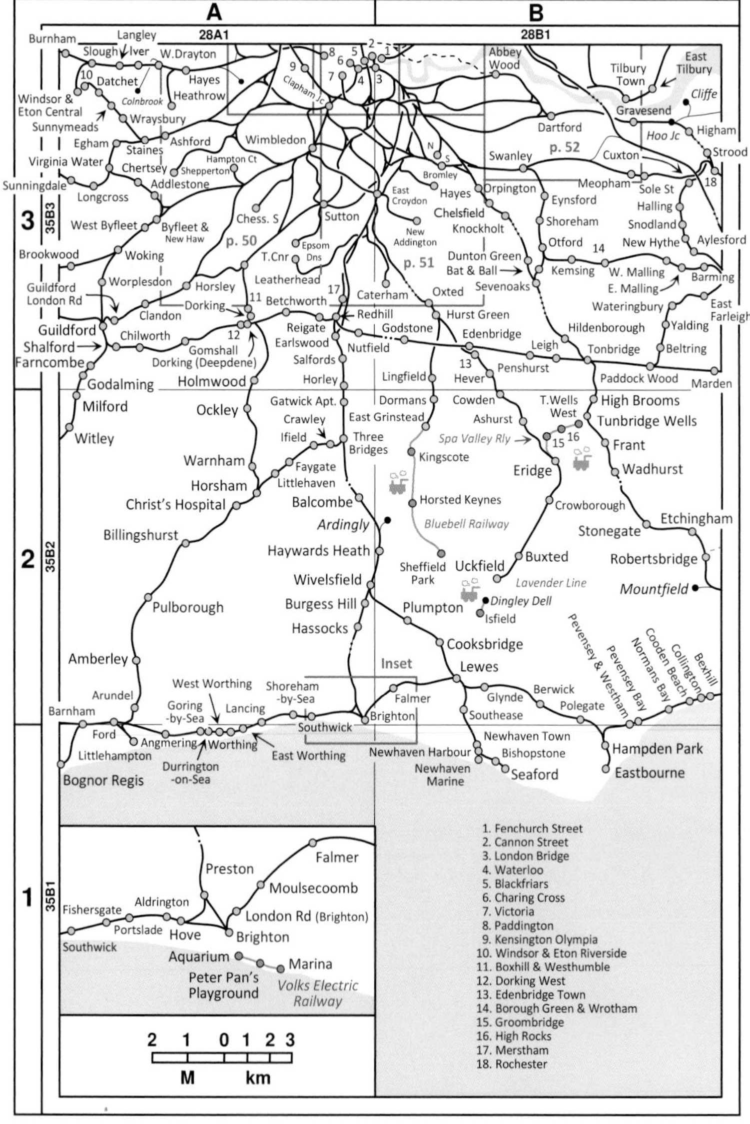

A
28A1

B
28B1

Burnham
Langley
Slough Iver W.Drayton
Datchet Colnbrook Hayes Heathrow
Windsor & 10 Wraysbury
Eton Central
Sunnymeads Egham Ashford Wimbledon
Windsor & Staines Hampton Ct
Eton Central Chertsey Shepperton
Virginia Water Addlestone
Sunningdale Longcross
West Byfleet Byfleet &
New Haw
Brookwood Woking
Guildford Worplesdon
London Rd
Clandon
Guildford Chilworth
Shalford
Farncombe

Abbey
Wood
Tilbury East
Town Tilbury
Gravesend Cliffe
Hoo Jc Higham
Dartford Strood
Swanley Cuxton Sole St 18
Meopham Halling
Chelsfield Eynsford Snodland New Hythe
Drpington Shoreham Aylesford
Hayes Otford 14 W. Malling Barming
Knockholt Kemsing E. Malling East
Dunton Green Wateringbury Farleigh
Bat & Ball Hildenborough Yalding
Sevenoaks Tonbridge Beltring
Penshurst Paddock Wood Marden

9
8 6 5
7 4 3
Clapham J
N
Bromley
East
Croydon
New
Addington

Sutton
Epsom
Dns
T.Cnr
Leatherhead
Betchworth 17
Reigate
Earlswood
Dorking (Deepdene) Salfords
Holmwood Horley

Caterham
Redhill
Godstone
Nutfield
Lingfield
Hurst Green
Edenbridge
Leigh
Hever 13

Godalming
Milford
Witley
Warnham
Horsham
Christ's Hospital
Billingshurst
Pulborough
Amberley
Arundel
Barnham
Ford
Littlehampton
Bognor Regis

Ockley
Crawley
Ifield
Faygate
Littlehaven
Balcombe
Ardingly
Haywards Heath
Wivelsfield
Burgess Hill
Hassocks

Gatwick Apt.
East Grinstead
Three
Bridges
Kingscote
Horsted Keynes
Sheffield
Park
Plumpton

Dormans
Cowden
Ashurst
Spa Valley Rly
15 16
Eridge
Bluebell Railway
Uckfield
Lavender Line
Dingley Dell
Isfield

T.Wells
West
Ashurst
Frant
Wadhurst
Crowborough
Buxted
Etchingham
Stonegate
Robertsbridge
Mountfield
High Brooms
Tunbridge Wells

Cooksbridge
Lewes
West Worthing Shoreham
Goring Lancing -by-Sea
-by-Sea Southwick
Angmering Worthing Brighton
Durrington East Worthing
-on-Sea
Falmer
Southease
Newhaven Town
Newhaven Harbour
Newhaven
Marine
Seaford
Berwick
Glynde Polegate
Bishopstone
Eastbourne
Hampden Park
Pevensey & Westham
Pevensey Bay
Cooden Beach
Normans Bay
Collington
Bexhill

Inset

Preston Falmer
Moulsecoomb
Aldrington
Fishersgate London Rd (Brighton)
Portslade Hove Brighton
Southwick
Aquarium Marina
Peter Pan's Volks Electric
Playground Railway

2 1 0 1 2 3
M   km

1. Fenchurch Street
2. Cannon Street
3. London Bridge
4. Waterloo
5. Blackfriars
6. Charing Cross
7. Victoria
8. Paddington
9. Kensington Olympia
10. Windsor & Eton Riverside
11. Boxhill & Westhumble
12. Dorking West
13. Edenbridge Town
14. Borough Green & Wrotham
15. Groombridge
16. High Rocks
17. Merstham
18. Rochester

p. 52
p. 50
p. 51

35B3
35B2
35B1

36

M 15   10   5   0   5   10   15   20 km

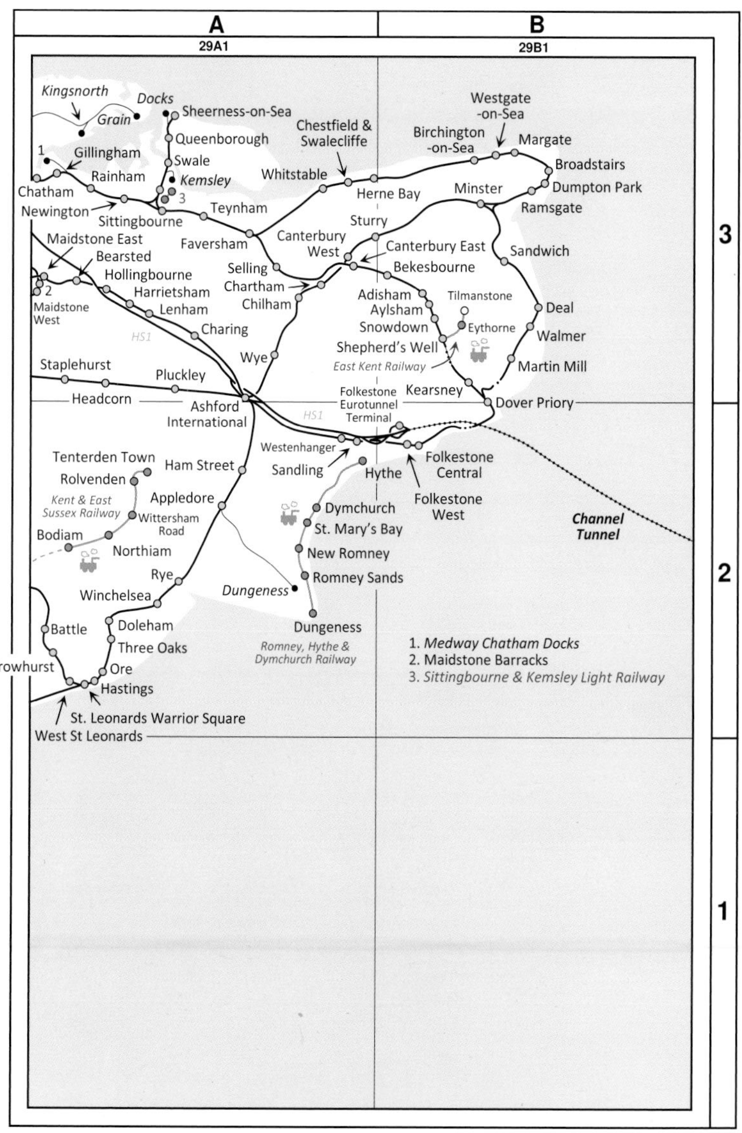

Kingsnorth
Docks
Grain
1
Gillingham
Chatham
Rainham
Newington
Sittingbourne
Sheerness-on-Sea
Queenborough
Swale
Kemsley
3
Whitstable
Teynham
Chestfield & Swalecliffe
Herne Bay
Sturry
Westgate -on-Sea
Birchington -on-Sea
Margate
Broadstairs
Dumpton Park
Minster
Ramsgate
Maidstone East
Bearsted
Hollingbourne
Harrietsham
Lenham
2
Maidstone West
HS1
Faversham
Selling
Chartham
Chilham
Charing
Wye
Canterbury West
Canterbury East
Bekesbourne
Adisham
Aylsham
Snowdown
Shepherd's Well
East Kent Railway
Sandwich
Tilmanstone
Eythorne
Deal
Walmer
Martin Mill
Staplehurst
Pluckley
Headcorn
Ashford International
HS1
Folkestone
Eurotunnel
Terminal
Kearsney
Dover Priory
Tenterden Town
Rolvenden
Kent & East
Sussex Railway
Bodiam
Wittersham
Road
Northiam
Rye
Winchelsea
Battle
Doleham
Three Oaks
Crowhurst
Ore
Hastings
St. Leonards Warrior Square
West St Leonards
Ham Street
Appledore
Westenhanger
Sandling
Hythe
Folkestone
Central
Folkestone
West
Dymchurch
St. Mary's Bay
New Romney
Romney Sands
Dungeness
Dungeness
Romney, Hythe &
Dymchurch Railway
Channel
Tunnel

1. *Medway Chatham Docks*
2. Maidstone Barracks
3. *Sittingbourne & Kemsley Light Railway*

3

2

1

M 15   10   5   0   5   10   15   20 km

37

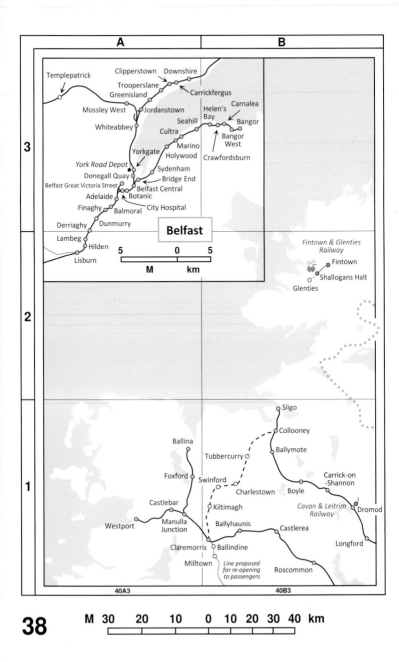

A

B

Templepatrick

Clipperstown
Downshire

Trooperslane
Greenisland
Carrickfergus

Mossley West
Jordanstown

Whiteabbey

Helen's
Bay
Carnalea

Seahill
Bangor

Cultra
Bangor
West

Marino
Crawfordsburn

Holywood

Yorkgate

Sydenham

York Road Depot

Donegall Quay
Bridge End

Belfast Great Victoria Street
Belfast Central

Adelaide
Botanic

Finaghy
Balmoral

City Hospital

Derriaghy
Dunmurry

Lambeg

Hilden

Lisburn

Belfast

5   0   5

M   km

3

*Fintown & Glenties
Railway*

Fintown

Shallogans Halt

Glenties

2

Sligo

Colloney

Ballina

Ballymote

Tubbercurry

Foxford
Swinford

Carrick-on
-Shannon

Charlestown
Boyle

Castlebar

Kiltimagh

*Cavan & Leitrim
Railway*

Dromod

Westport
Manulla
Junction

Ballyhaunis

Castlerea

Longford

1

Claremorris
Ballindine

Milltown
*Line proposed
for re-opening
to passengers*

Roscommon

40A3

40B3

38

M 30   20   10   0   10   20   30   40 km

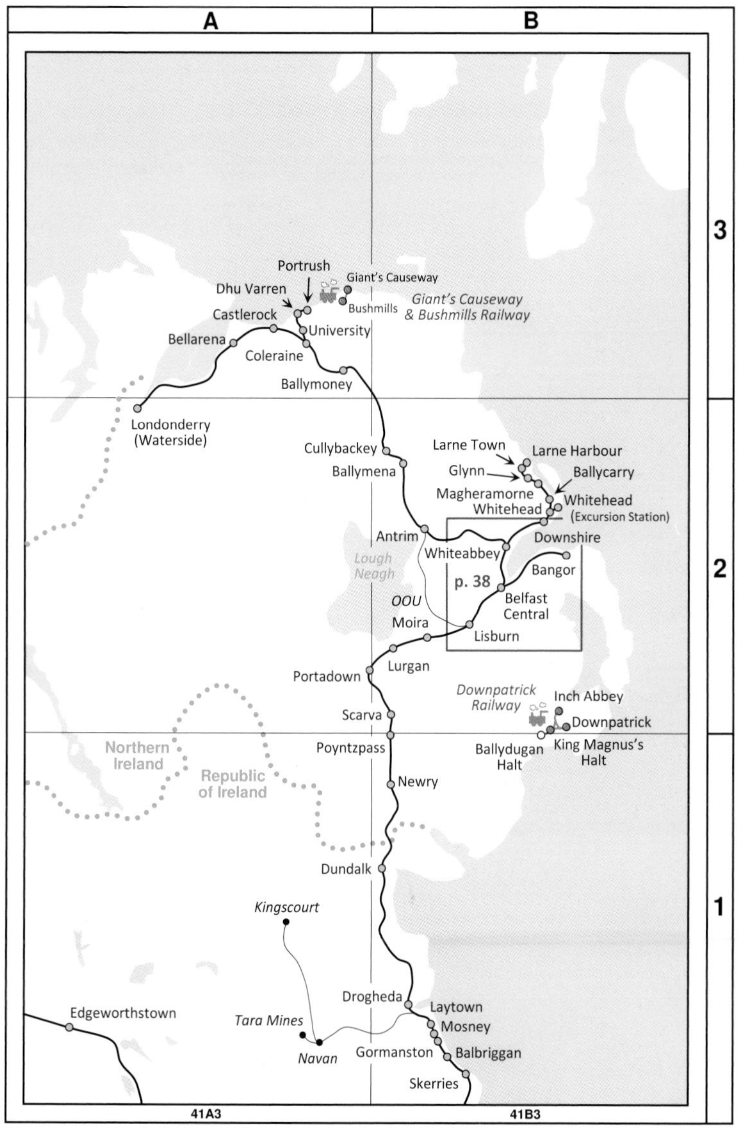

	A	B	

3

Portrush
Dhu Varren
Castlerock
Bellarena
Coleraine
University
Ballymoney

Giant's Causeway
Bushmills

Giant's Causeway & Bushmills Railway

Londonderry
(Waterside)

2

Cullybackey
Ballymena

Larne Town
Glynn
Magheramorne
Whitehead

Larne Harbour
Ballycarry
Whitehead
(Excursion Station)

Antrim

Whiteabbey
Lough Neagh

Downshire
Bangor

OOU
Moira

p. 38

Belfast
Central

Lisburn

Portadown
Lurgan

Downpatrick Railway

Inch Abbey
Downpatrick

Scarva

Ballydugan
Halt

King Magnus's
Halt

Northern Ireland

Poyntzpass

Republic of Ireland

Newry

1

Dundalk

Kingscourt

Edgeworthstown

Tara Mines

Navan

Drogheda
Laytown
Mosney
Gormanston
Balbriggan
Skerries

41A3

41B3

M 30 20 10 0 10 20 30 40 km

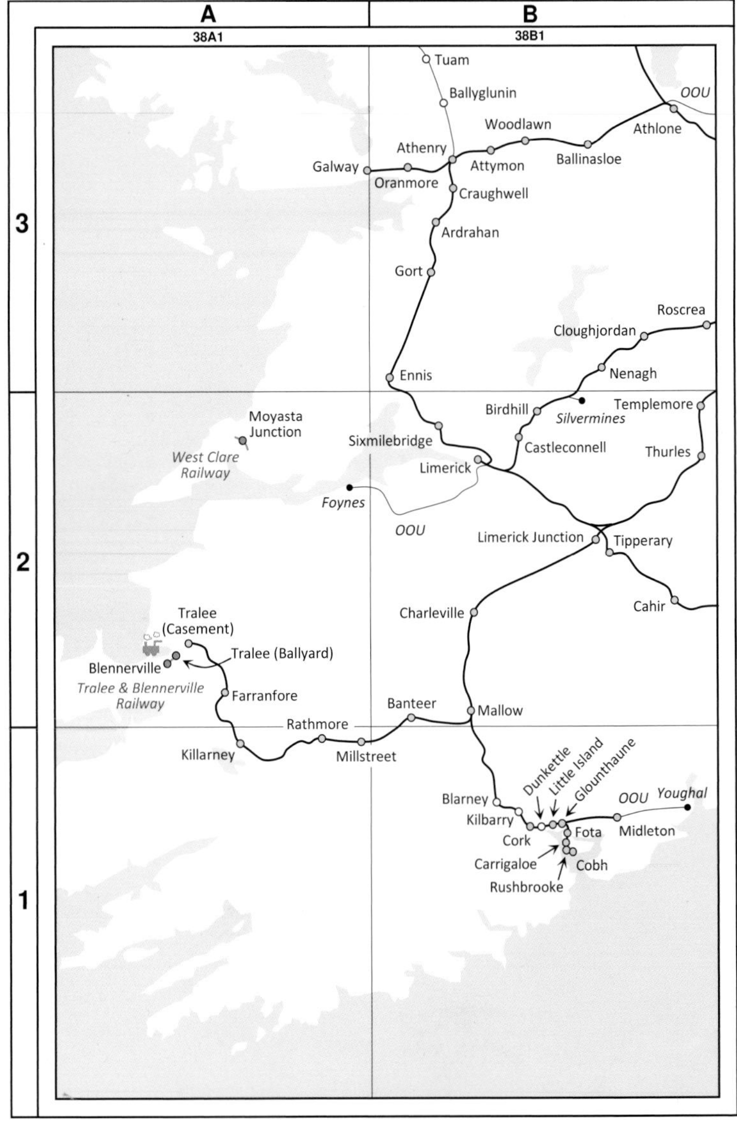

	A	B
	38A1	38B1

Tuam
Ballyglunin
Woodlawn
OOU
Athlone
Athenry
Attymon
Ballinasloe
Galway
Oranmore
Craughwell
Ardrahan
Gort
Roscrea
Cloughjordan
Nenagh

3

Ennis
Birdhill
Templemore
Silvermines
Moyasta Junction
Sixmilebridge
Castleconnell
Thurles
West Clare Railway
Limerick
Foynes
OOU
Limerick Junction
Tipperary
Cahir

2

Charleville
Tralee (Casement)
Tralee (Ballyard)
Blennerville
Tralee & Blennerville Railway
Farranfore
Banteer
Mallow
Rathmore
Killarney
Millstreet
Dunkettle
Little Island
Glounthaune
OOU
Youghal
Blarney
Kilbarry
Fota
Midleton
Cork
Carrigaloe
Cobh
Rushbrooke

1

40   M 30   20   10   0   10 20 30 40 km

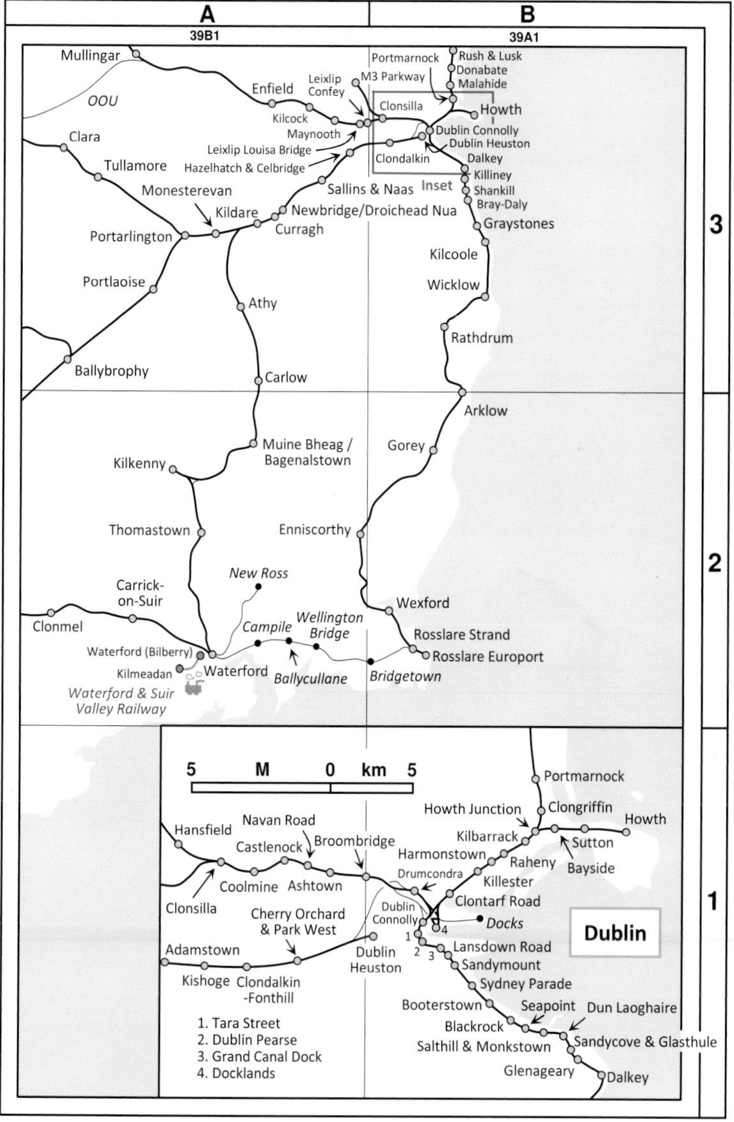

Mullingar
OOU
Enfield
Leixlip Confey
Portmarnock
M3 Parkway
Rush & Lusk
Donabate
Malahide
Clonsilla
Howth
Kilcock
Maynooth
Dublin Connolly
Dublin Heuston
Clondalkin
Dalkey
Killiney
Shankill
Bray-Daly
Clara
Tullamore
Leixlip Louisa Bridge
Hazelhatch & Celbridge
Monesterevan
Sallins & Naas
Inset
Kildare
Newbridge/Droichead Nua
Graystones
Curragh
Portarlington
Kilcoole
Portlaoise
Wicklow
Athy
Rathdrum
Ballybrophy
Carlow

3

Arklow

Muine Bheag / Bagenalstown
Kilkenny
Gorey

Thomastown
Enniscorthy

Carrick-on-Suir
New Ross
Wexford

Clonmel
Campile
Wellington Bridge
Rosslare Strand
Rosslare Europort
Waterford (Bilberry)
Kilmeadan
Waterford
Ballycullane
Bridgetown
Waterford & Suir Valley Railway

2

5   M   0   km   5

Hansfield
Navan Road
Castlenock
Broombridge
Portmarnock
Howth Junction
Clongriffin
Howth
Kilbarrack
Sutton
Harmonstown
Raheny
Bayside
Drumcondra
Killester
Coolmine
Ashtown
Clontarf Road
Clonsilla
Cherry Orchard & Park West
Dublin Connolly
Docks
Dublin
Adamstown
1
4
2 3
Lansdown Road
Dublin Heuston
Sandymount
Kishoge
Clondalkin-Fonthill
Sydney Parade
Booterstown
Seapoint
Dun Laoghaire
Blackrock
Salthill & Monkstown
Sandycove & Glasthule
Glenageary
Dalkey

1. Tara Street
2. Dublin Pearse
3. Grand Canal Dock
4. Docklands

1

M 30   20   10   0   10   20   30   40 km

41

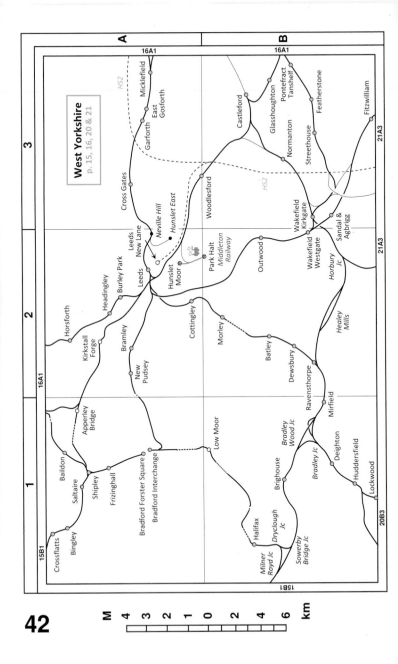

West Yorkshire
p. 15, 16, 20 & 21

42

16A1

16A1

15B1

21A3

21A3

20B3

15B1

Micklefield
East Gosforth
Garforth
Cross Gates
Neville Hill
Hunslet East
Leeds New Lane
Burley Park
Leeds
Hunslet Moor
Park Halt
Middleton Railway
Headingley
Horsforth
Kirkstall Forge
Bramley
New Pudsey
Cottingley
Morley
Batley
Dewsbury
Ravensthorpe
Mirfield
Apperley Bridge
Low Moor
Bradford Forster Square
Bradford Interchange
Baildon
Saltaire
Shipley
Frizinghall
Crossflatts
Bingley
Brighouse
Bradley Wood Jc
Bradley Jc
Deighton
Huddersfield
Lockwood
Halifax
Dryclough Jc
Milner Royd Jc
Sowerby Bridge Jc

Woodlesford
Castleford
Glasshoughton
Pontefract Tanshelf
Featherstone
Fitzwilliam
Normanton
Streethouse
Wakefield Kirkgate
Sandal & Agbrigg
Wakefield Westgate
Horbury Jc
Outwood
Healey Mills

HS2

HS2

M
4
3
2
1
0
2
4
6
km

A

B

3

2

1

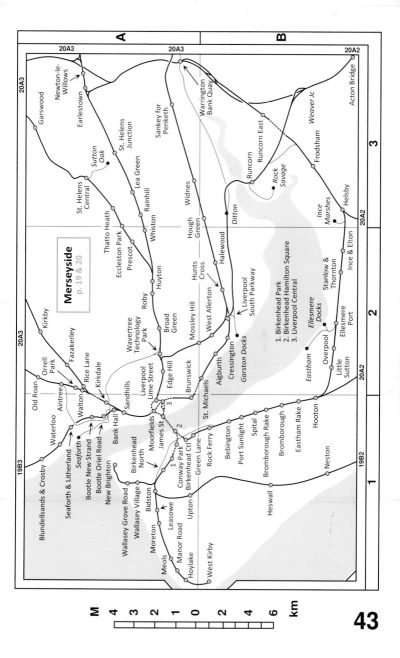

A

B

20A3 — 20A3 — 20A2

Garswood
Newton-le-Willows
Earlestown
St. Helens Junction
Sankey for Penketh
Warrington Bank Quay
Acton Bridge
Weaver Jc
3

St. Helens Central
Sutton Oak
Lea Green
Rainhill
Sutton Oak
Runcorn East
Runcorn
Rock Savage
Frodsham
Helsby
Ince Marshes
20A2

20A3

Thatto Heath
Eccleston Park
Prescot
Whiston
Hough Green
Widnes
Ditton

Kirkby
Wavertree Technology Park
Roby
Huyton
Broad Green
Mossley Hill
West Allerton
Hunts Cross
Halewood
Liverpool South Parkway

Ince & Elton

Fazakerley
Rice Lane
Kirkdale
Mossley Hill
Edge Hill
Brunswick
St. Michaels
Aigburth
Cressington
Garston Docks
Liverpool Hamilton Square
Liverpool Central
Birkenhead Park

Stanlow & Thornton
Ellesmere Docks
Ellesmere Port
Overpool
Eastham

20A2

Orrell Park
Old Roan
Walton
Aintree
Bank Hall
Sandhills
Liverpool Lime Street
Moorfields
James St
3
2
1. Birkenhead Park
2. Birkenhead Hamilton Square
3. Liverpool Central

Little Sutton

Waterloo
Seaforth & Litherland
Bootle New Strand
Bootle Oriel Road
New Brighton
Seaforth
Birkenhead North
Conway Park
Birkenhead Ctr
Green Lane
Rock Ferry
Bebington
Port Sunlight
Spital
Bromborough Rake
Bromborough
Eastham Rake
Hooton
Neston

19B3

Blundellsands & Crosby

Wallasey Grove Road
Wallasey Village
Moreton
Bidston
Leasowe
Upton
Manor Road
Meols
Hoylake
West Kirby
Heswall

19B2

Merseyside
p. 19 & 20

M
4
3
2
1
0
2
4
6
km

43

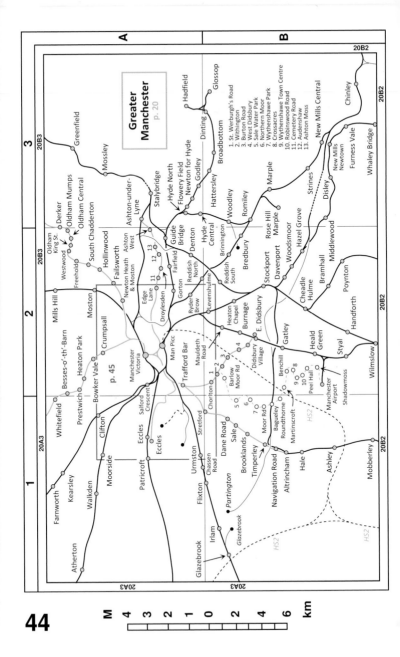

44

Greater Manchester
p. 20

1. St. Werburgh's Road
2. Withington
3. Burton Road
4. West Didsbury
5. Sale Water Park
6. Northern Moor
7. Wythenshawe Park
8. Crossacres
9. Wythenshawe Town Centre
10. Robinswood Road
11. Cemetery Road
12. Audenshaw
13. Ashton Moss

M 4 3 2 1 0 2 4 6 km

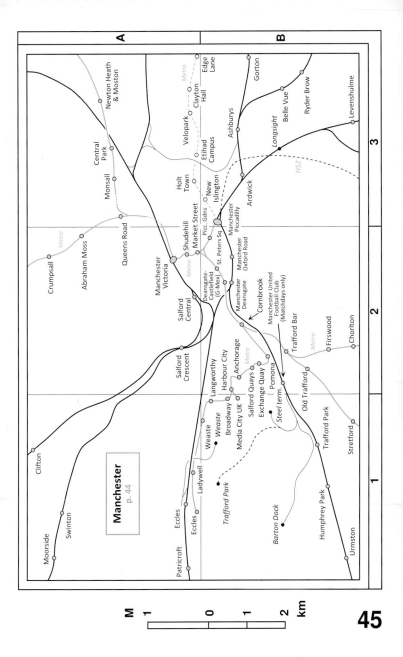

Manchester
p. 44

A

B

Clifton
Moorside
Swinton

Patricroft
Eccles
Eccles
Ladywell
Weaste
Weaste
Broadway
Langworthy
Harbour City
Media City UK
Salford Quays
Exchange Quay
Pomona
Steel term.
Anchorage
Trafford Park
Barton Dock
Humphrey Park
Trafford Park
Stretford
Urmston

Salford Crescent
Salford Central
Manchester Victoria
Queens Road
Abraham Moss
Crumpsall

Central Park
Monsall
Newton Heath & Moston

Deansgate-Castlefield (G-Mex)
Manchester Deansgate
Cornbrook
Manchester United Football Club (Matchdays only)
Old Trafford
Trafford Bar
Firswood
Chorlton

St. Peters Sq
Manchester Oxford Road
Shudehill
Market Street
Picc. Gdns
New Islington
Holt Town
Velopark
Etihad Campus
Clayton Hall
Edge Lane

Manchester Piccadilly
Ardwick
Ashburys
Longsight
Gorton
Belle Vue
Ryder Brow
Levenshulme

HS2

Metro

M
1
0
1
2
km

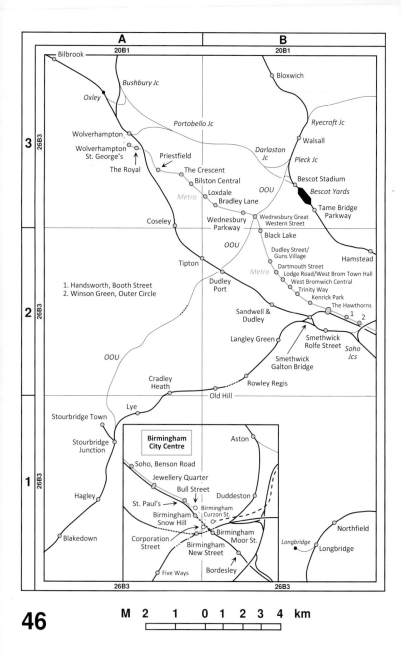

A

20B1

B

20B1

Bilbrook

Bloxwich

Bushbury Jc

Oxley

Portobello Jc

Ryecroft Jc

3

26B3

Wolverhampton

Walsall

Wolverhampton
St. George's

Priestfield

Darlaston
Jc

Pleck Jc

The Royal

The Crescent

Bescot Stadium

Bilston Central

OOU

Bescot Yards

Metro

Loxdale
Bradley Lane

Tame Bridge
Parkway

Coseley

Wednesbury
Parkway

Wednesbury Great
Western Street

Black Lake

OOU

Dudley Street/
Guns Village

Hamstead

Tipton

Metro

Dartmouth Street
Lodge Road/West Brom Town Hall
West Bromwich Central
Trinity Way
Kenrick Park

1. Handsworth, Booth Street
2. Winson Green, Outer Circle

Dudley Port

The Hawthorns

2

26B3

Sandwell &
Dudley

1 2

Langley Green

Smethwick
Rolfe Street

Soho
Jcs

OOU

Smethwick
Galton Bridge

Cradley
Heath

Rowley Regis

Lye

Old Hill

Stourbridge Town

Birmingham
City Centre

Aston

Stourbridge
Junction

Soho, Benson Road

Jewellery Quarter

Bull Street

1

26B3

Hagley

St. Paul's

Duddeston

Birmingham
Snow Hill

Birmingham
Curzon St.

Northfield

Corporation
Street

Birmingham
Moor St.

Longbridge

Longbridge

Blakedown

Birmingham
New Street

Five Ways

Bordesley

26B3

26B3

46

M 2   1   0   1   2   3   4   km

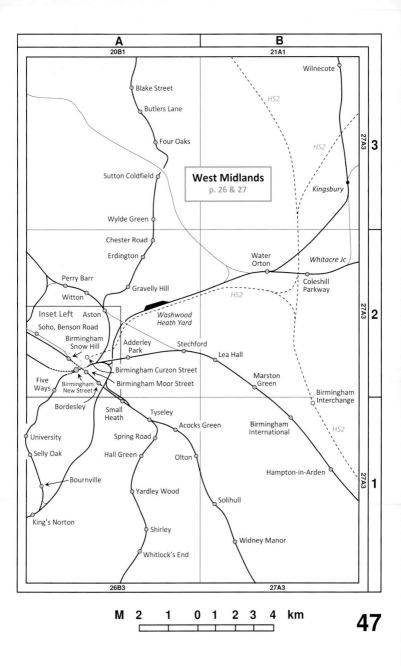

Wilnecote

HS2

Blake Street

Butlers Lane

HS2

27A3

3

Four Oaks

Sutton Coldfield

West Midlands
p. 26 & 27

Kingsbury

Wylde Green

Chester Road

Erdington

Water
Orton

Whitacre Jc

Perry Barr

Gravelly Hill

Coleshill
Parkway

Witton

Inset Left   Aston

*Washwood
Heath Yard*

HS2

27A3

2

Soho, Benson Road

Birmingham Snow Hill

Adderley
Park

Stechford

Lea Hall

Marston
Green

Birmingham Curzon Street

Five
Ways

Birmingham
New Street

Birmingham Moor Street

Birmingham
Interchange

Bordesley

Small
Heath

Tyseley

Acocks Green

Birmingham
International

HS2

27A3

1

University

Spring Road

Selly Oak

Hall Green

Olton

Bournville

Yardley Wood

Solihull

Hampton-in-Arden

King's Norton

Shirley

Widney Manor

Whitlock's End

M 2   1   0   1   2   3   4   km

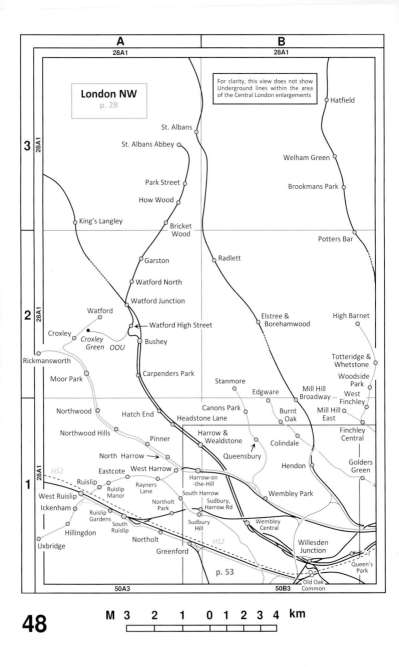

28A1
28A1

London NW
p. 28

For clarity, this view does not show Underground lines within the area of the Central London enlargements

Hatfield

St. Albans

St. Albans Abbey

3   Welham Green

Brookmans Park

Park Street

How Wood

King's Langley

Bricket Wood

Potters Bar

Garston

Radlett

Watford North

Watford Junction

Watford

Elstree & Borehamwood

High Barnet

Croxley

Watford High Street

Croxley Green   OOU

Bushey

Totteridge & Whetstone

Rickmansworth

Woodside Park

West Finchley

Moor Park

Carpenders Park

Stanmore

Edgware

Mill Hill Broadway

Mill Hill East

Northwood

Hatch End

Canons Park

Headstone Lane

Burnt Oak

Finchley Central

Northwood Hills

Pinner

Harrow & Wealdstone

Colindale

Golders Green

North Harrow

West Harrow

Queensbury

Hendon

HS2

Eastcote

Ruislip

Rayners Lane

Harrow-on-the-Hill

Ruislip Manor

South Harrow

Sudbury, Harrow Rd

Wembley Park

West Ruislip

Ickenham

Ruislip Gardens

Northolt Park

Sudbury Hill

Wembley Central

South Ruislip

Willesden Junction

Hillingdon

Northolt

Queen's Park

Uxbridge

Greenford

HS2

p. 53

Old Oak Common

M 3 2 1 0 1 2 3 4 km

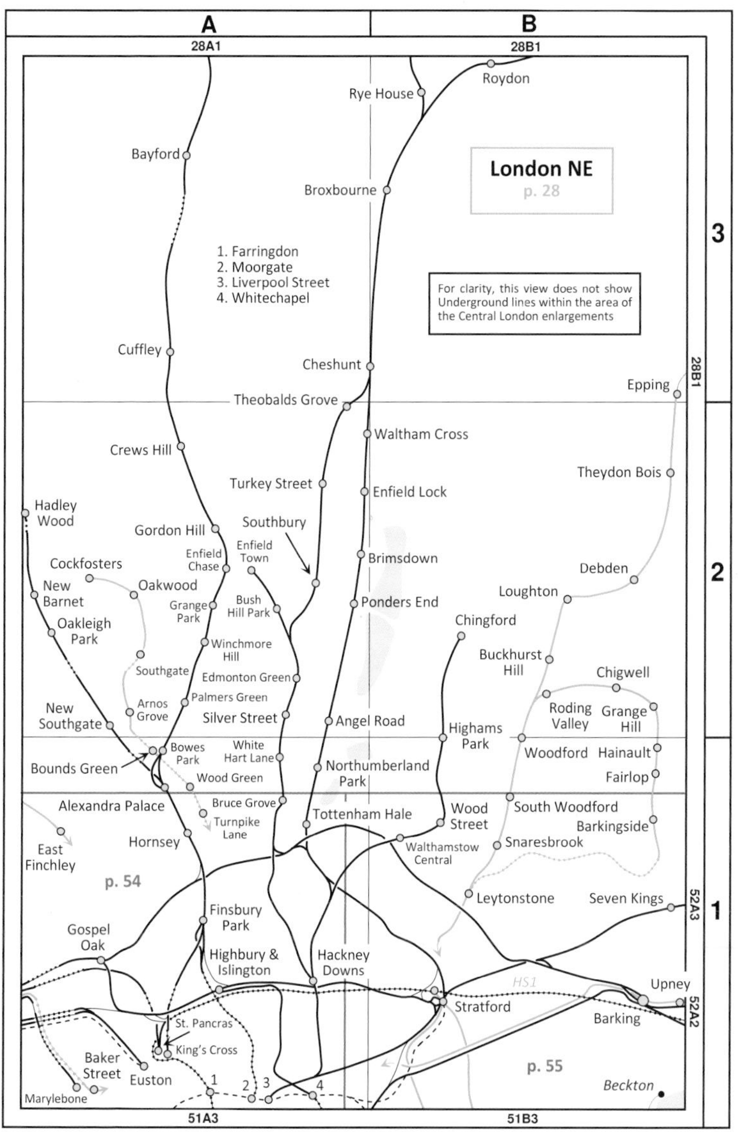

A	B

28A1 28B1

Roydon

Rye House

Bayford

Broxbourne

London NE
p. 28

1. Farringdon
2. Moorgate
3. Liverpool Street
4. Whitechapel

For clarity, this view does not show
Underground lines within the area of
the Central London enlargements

Cuffley

Cheshunt

Epping

28B1

Theobalds Grove

Waltham Cross

Crews Hill

Theydon Bois

Turkey Street

Enfield Lock

Hadley
Wood

Gordon Hill

Southbury

Brimsdown

Debden

Enfield
Chase

Enfield
Town

Loughton

Cockfosters

New
Barnet

Oakwood

Grange
Park

Bush
Hill Park

Ponders End

Chingford

Oakleigh
Park

Winchmore
Hill

Buckhurst
Hill

Chigwell

Edmonton Green

Southgate

Palmers Green

New
Southgate

Arnos
Grove

Silver Street

Angel Road

Roding
Valley

Grange
Hill

Highams
Park

Hainault

Bowes
Park

White
Hart Lane

Woodford

Fairlop

Bounds Green

Wood Green

Northumberland
Park

Alexandra Palace

Bruce Grove

Tottenham Hale

Wood
Street

South Woodford

Barkingside

Turnpike
Lane

Hornsey

Walthamstow
Central

Snaresbrook

East
Finchley

p. 54

Leytonstone

Seven Kings

52A3

Finsbury
Park

Gospel
Oak

Highbury &
Islington

Hackney
Downs

Upney

St. Pancras

HS1

Stratford

52A2

Baker
Street

King's Cross

Barking

Marylebone

Euston

1   2 3   4

p. 55

Beckton

51A3 51B3

M 3   2   1   0   1   2   3   4   km

49

3

2

1

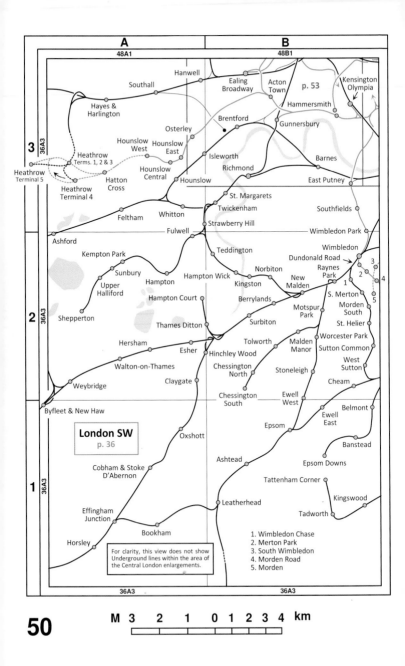

Hanwell

Southall

Ealing
Broadway

Acton
Town

p. 53

Kensington
Olympia

Hayes &
Harlington

Hammersmith

Osterley

Brentford

Gunnersbury

Hounslow
West

Hounslow
East

Isleworth

Barnes

3

Heathrow
Terms. 1, 2 & 3

Hounslow
Central

Richmond

Heathrow
Terminal 5

Hatton
Cross

Hounslow

East Putney

Heathrow
Terminal 4

St. Margarets

Feltham

Whitton

Twickenham

Southfields

Ashford

Fulwell

Strawberry Hill

Wimbledon Park

Kempton Park

Teddington

Wimbledon

Dundonald Road

Sunbury

Hampton Wick

Norbiton

Raynes
Park

3

Upper
Halliford

Hampton

Kingston

New
Malden

2

1

4

Hampton Court

Berrylands

S. Merton

5

Shepperton

Surbiton

Motspur
Park

Morden
South

Thames Ditton

Tolworth

Malden
Manor

St. Helier

Hersham

Esher

Hinchley Wood

Worcester Park

Walton-on-Thames

Chessington
North

Stoneleigh

Sutton Common

Weybridge

Claygate

West
Sutton

Byfleet & New Haw

Chessington
South

Ewell
West

Cheam

London SW
p. 36

Oxshott

Epsom

Ewell
East

Belmont

Ashtead

Banstead

Cobham & Stoke
D'Abernon

Epsom Downs

Tattenham Corner

Effingham
Junction

Leatherhead

Kingswood

Bookham

Tadworth

Horsley

1. Wimbledon Chase
2. Merton Park
3. South Wimbledon
4. Morden Road
5. Morden

For clarity, this view does not show
Underground lines within the area of
the Central London enlargements.

1

M 3 2 1 0 1 2 3 4 km

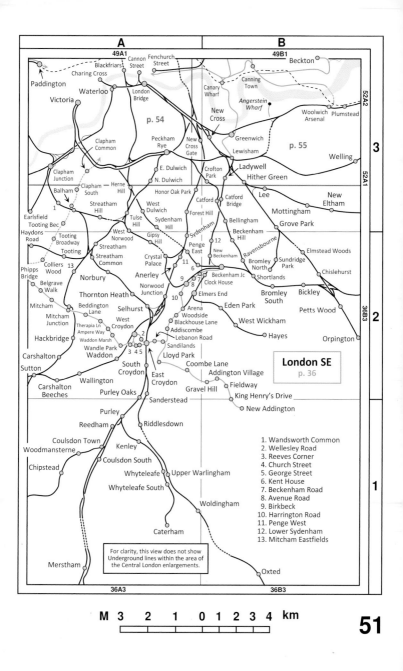

London SE
p. 36

1. Wandsworth Common
2. Wellesley Road
3. Reeves Corner
4. Church Street
5. George Street
6. Kent House
7. Beckenham Road
8. Avenue Road
9. Birkbeck
10. Harrington Road
11. Penge West
12. Lower Sydenham
13. Mitcham Eastfields

For clarity, this view does not show Underground lines within the area of the Central London enlargements.

M 3 2 1 0 1 2 3 4 km

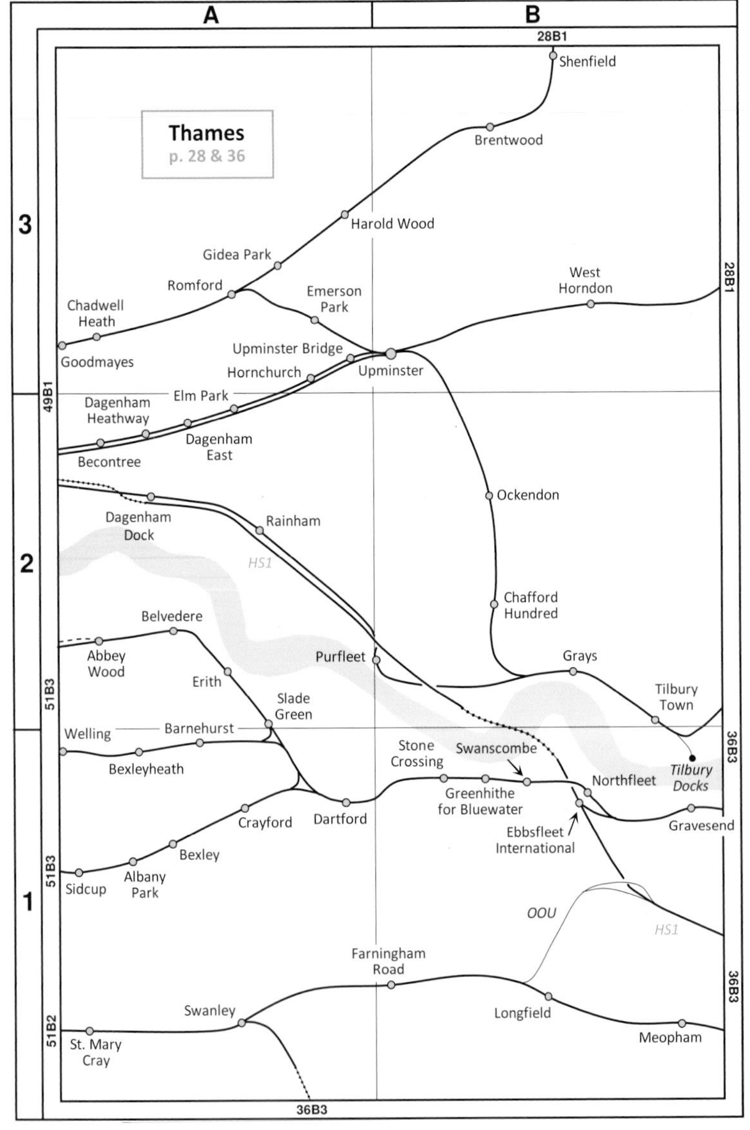

Thames
p. 28 & 36

28B1

Shenfield

Brentwood

Harold Wood

West
Horndon

Gidea Park

Romford

Emerson
Park

Chadwell
Heath

Goodmayes

Upminster Bridge

Hornchurch

Upminster

Elm Park

Dagenham
Heathway

Becontree

Dagenham
East

Ockendon

Dagenham
Dock

Rainham

HS1

Chafford
Hundred

Belvedere

Abbey
Wood

Erith

Slade
Green

Purfleet

Grays

Tilbury
Town

Welling

Barnehurst

Bexleyheath

Stone
Crossing

Swanscombe

Northfleet

*Tilbury
Docks*

Greenhithe
for Bluewater

Crayford

Dartford

Ebbsfleet
International

Gravesend

Bexley

Albany
Park

Sidcup

OOU

HS1

Farningham
Road

Swanley

Longfield

Meopham

St. Mary
Cray

36B3

49B1

51B3

51B3

51B2

28B1

36B3

36B3

52

M 3 2 1 0 1 2 3 4 km

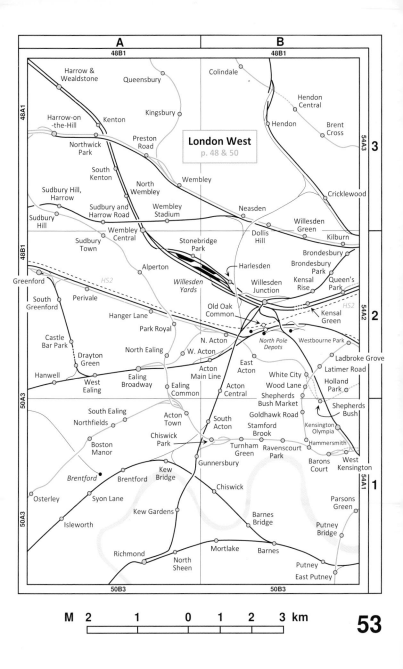

London West
p. 48 & 50

Harrow &
Wealdstone

Queensbury

Colindale

Hendon
Central

Harrow-on
-the-Hill

Kenton

Kingsbury

Hendon

Brent
Cross

Northwick
Park

Preston
Road

South
Kenton

North
Wembley

Wembley

Neasden

Cricklewood

Sudbury Hill,
Harrow

Sudbury and
Harrow Road

Wembley
Stadium

Willesden
Green

Kilburn

Sudbury
Hill

Wembley
Central

Dollis
Hill

Brondesbury

Sudbury
Town

Stonebridge
Park

Harlesden

Brondesbury
Park

Alperton

*Willesden
Yards*

Willesden
Junction

Kensal
Rise

Queen's
Park

Greenford

South
Greenford

Perivale

HS2

Old Oak
Common

Kensal
Green

HS2

Castle
Bar Park

Hanger Lane

Park Royal

N. Acton

*North Pole
Depots*

Westbourne Park

Ladbroke Grove

Drayton
Green

North Ealing

W. Acton

East
Acton

Latimer Road

Hanwell

West
Ealing

Ealing
Broadway

Ealing
Common

Acton
Main Line

Acton
Central

White City

Wood
Lane

Holland
Park

Shepherds
Bush

South Ealing

Northfields

Acton
Town

South
Acton

Shepherds
Bush Market

Goldhawk Road

Stamford
Brook

Kensington
Olympia

Boston
Manor

Chiswick
Park

Turnham
Green

Ravenscourt
Park

Hammersmith

Brentford

Brentford

Kew
Bridge

Gunnersbury

Barons
Court

West
Kensington

Osterley

Syon Lane

Chiswick

Parsons
Green

Kew Gardens

Putney
Bridge

Isleworth

Barnes
Bridge

Richmond

North
Sheen

Mortlake

Barnes

Putney

East Putney

M 2 1 0 1 2 3 km

53

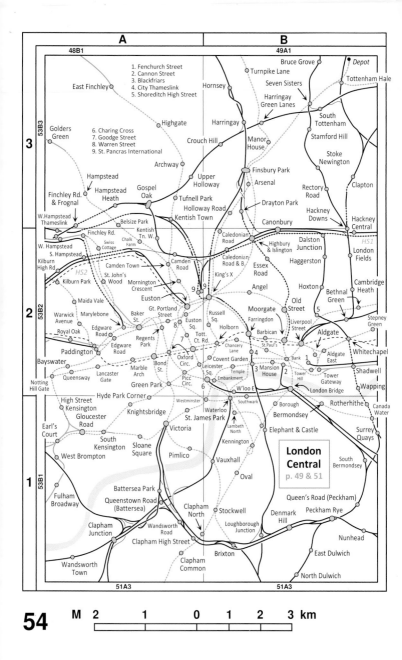

1. Fenchurch Street
2. Cannon Street
3. Blackfriars
4. City Thameslink
5. Shoreditch High Street

6. Charing Cross
7. Goodge Street
8. Warren Street
9. St. Pancras International

53B3

3

East Finchley
Golders Green
Highgate
Hampstead
Finchley Rd. & Frognal
Hampstead Heath
Gospel Oak
Belsize Park
W. Hampstead Thameslink
Finchley Rd.

Hornsey
Turnpike Lane
Bruce Grove
Seven Sisters
Tottenham Hale
Depot
Harringay Green Lanes
South Tottenham
Harringay
Stamford Hill
Crouch Hill
Manor House
Stoke Newington
Archway
Upper Holloway
Finsbury Park
Clapton
Arsenal
Rectory Road
Hackney Downs
Tufnell Park
Holloway Road
Drayton Park
Hackney Central
Kentish Town
Canonbury
London Fields
HS1

53B2

2

W. Hampstead
S. Hampstead
Kilburn High Rd
HS2
Kilburn Park
Maida Vale
Warwick Avenue
Royal Oak
Paddington
Bayswater
Notting Hill Gate
Queensway
Lancaster Gate

Kentish Tn. W.
Swiss Cottage
Chalk Farm
Camden Town
Camden Road
St. John's Wood
Mornington Crescent
Euston
Marylebone
Baker St.
Gt. Portland Street
Edgware Road
Regents Park
Edgware Road
Marble Arch
Bond St.
Oxford Circ.
Green Park
Hyde Park Corner

Caledonian Road
Highbury & Islington
Dalston Junction
Haggerston
Essex Road
King's X
Angel
Hoxton
Bethnal Green
Cambridge Heath
9 9
Russell Sq.
Moorgate
Old Street
Stepney Green
8 8
Euston Sq.
Farringdon
Liverpool Street
7
Tott. Ct. Rd.
Holborn
Barbican
Aldgate
Whitechapel
Chancery Lane
St. Paul's
5
Covent Garden
4
Bank
Aldgate East
Leicester Sq.
3 Mansion House
2
Shadwell
Picc. Circ.
Temple
Tower Hill
Wapping
6
Embankment
W'loo E
Tower Gateway
London Bridge
Rotherhithe
Canada Water

53B1

1

Earl's Court
West Brompton
Fulham Broadway
High Street Kensington
Gloucester Road
Knightsbridge
St. James Park
Victoria
South Kensington
Sloane Square
Pimlico
Westminster
Waterloo
Southwark
Lambeth North
Kennington
Vauxhall
Oval
Borough
Bermondsey
Elephant & Castle
Surrey Quays
South Bermondsey

London Central
p. 49 & 51

Battersea Park
Queenstown Road (Battersea)
Clapham North
Stockwell
Queen's Road (Peckham)
Denmark Hill
Peckham Rye
Clapham Junction
Wandsworth Road
Loughborough Junction
Nunhead
Clapham High Street
East Dulwich
Wandsworth Town
Clapham Common
Brixton
North Dulwich

54

M 2 1 0 1 2 3 km

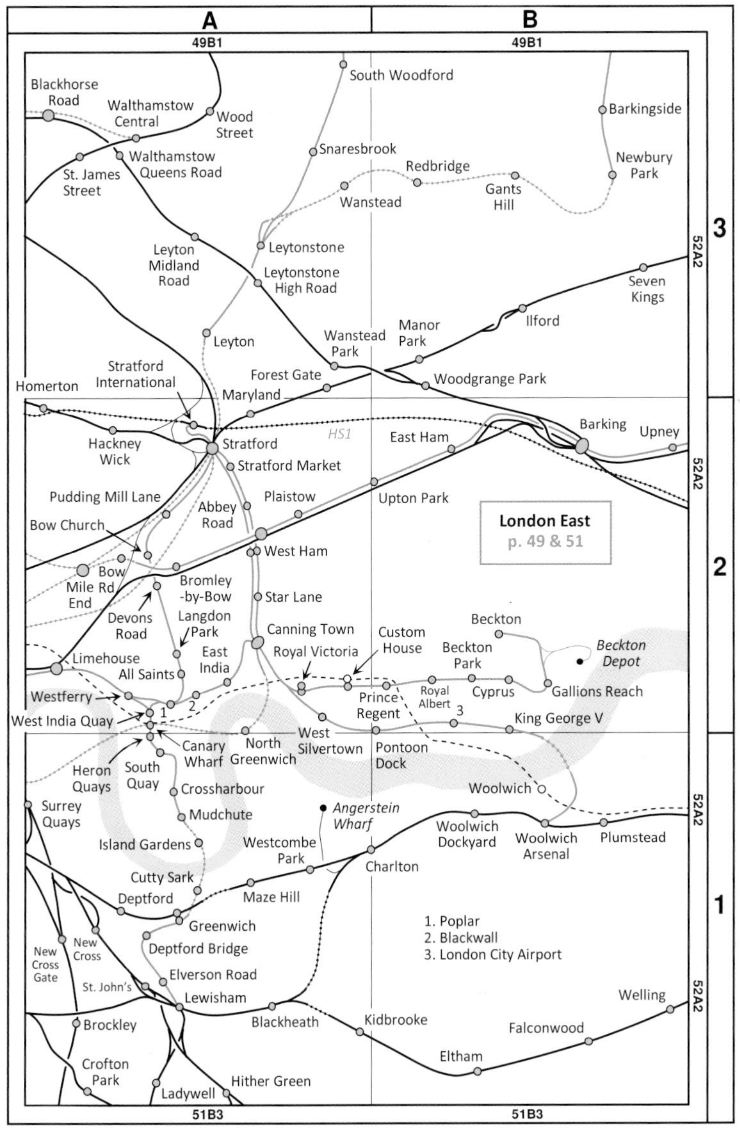

Blackhorse Road
Walthamstow Central
Wood Street
St. James Street
Walthamstow Queens Road
South Woodford
Barkingside
Snaresbrook
Redbridge
Newbury Park
Wanstead
Gants Hill
Leyton Midland Road
Leytonstone
Leytonstone High Road
Leyton
Wanstead Park
Manor Park
Ilford
Seven Kings
Homerton
Stratford International
Forest Gate
Maryland
Woodgrange Park
Hackney Wick
Stratford
HS1
East Ham
Barking
Upney
Stratford Market
Pudding Mill Lane
Plaistow
Upton Park
Bow Church
Abbey Road
London East
p. 49 & 51
Bow Mile Rd End
West Ham
Bromley-by-Bow
Star Lane
Beckton
Devons Road
Langdon Park
Beckton Park
Beckton Depot
Limehouse
East India
Canning Town
Royal Victoria
Custom House
Cyprus
Gallions Reach
Westferry
All Saints
Royal Albert 3
West India Quay
1
Prince Regent
King George V
Heron Quays
South Quay
Canary Wharf
North Greenwich
West Silvertown
Pontoon Dock
Woolwich
Surrey Quays
Crossharbour
Mudchute
Island Gardens
Westcombe Park
Angerstein Wharf
Woolwich Dockyard
Woolwich Arsenal
Plumstead
Cutty Sark
Deptford
Maze Hill
Charlton
Greenwich
New Cross
New Cross Gate
Deptford Bridge
Elverson Road
Lewisham
1. Poplar
2. Blackwall
3. London City Airport
St. John's
Brockley
Blackheath
Kidbrooke
Welling
Falconwood
Crofton Park
Eltham
Ladywell
Hither Green

M 2   1   0   1   2   3 km

55

Stations in Ireland

41A1	Adamstown	40B2	Castleconnell
38A3	Adelaide	41A1	Castlenock
39B2	Antrim	38B1	Castlerea
40B3	Ardrahan	39A3	Castlerock
41B2	Arklow	31B1	Charlestown
41A1	Ashtown	40B2	Charleville
40B3	Athenry	41A1	Cherry Orchard & Park West
40B3	Athlone	41B1	Christchurch (Dublin)
41A3	Athy	38A3	City Hospital
40B3	Attymon	41A3	Clara
39B1	Balbriggan	38B1	Claremorris
38A1	Ballina	38A3	Clipperstown
40B3	Ballinasloe	41A1	Clondalkin-Fonthill
38B1	Ballindine	41B1	Clongriffin
41A3	Ballybrophy	41A2	Clonmel
39B2	Ballycarry	41A1	Clonsilla
41A2	Ballycullane	41B1	Clontarf Road
39B1	Ballydugan Halt	40B3	Cloughjordan
40B3	Ballyglunin	40B1	Cobh
38B1	Ballyhaunis	39A3	Coleraine
39B2	Ballymena	38B1	Collooney
39A3	Ballymoney	41A1	Coolmine
38B1	Ballymote	40B1	Cork
38A3	Balmoral	40B3	Craughwell
38B3	Bangor (Northern Ireland)	38B3	Crawfordsburn
38B3	Bangor West	39B2	Cullybackey
40B2	Banteer	38A3	Cultra
41B1	Bayside	41A3	Curragh
38A3	Belfast Central	41B1	Dalkey
38A3	Belfast Great Victoria Street	38A3	Derriaghy
39A3	Bellarena	39A3	Dhu Varren
40B2	Birdhill	41B1	Docklands (4)
41B1	Blackrock	41B3	Donabate
40B1	Blarney	38A3	Donegall Quay
40A2	Blennerville	39B2	Downpatrick
41B1	Booterstown	38A3	Downshire
38A3	Botanic	39B1	Drogheda
38B1	Boyle	38B1	Dromod
41B3	Bray-Daly	41B1	Drumcondra
38A3	Bridge End	41B1	Dublin Connolly
41B2	Bridgetown	41B1	Dublin Docks
41A1	Broombridge	41B1	Dublin Heuston
39A3	Bushmills	41B1	Dublin Pearse (2)
40B2	Cahir	41B1	Dun Laoghaire
41A2	Campile	39B1	Dundalk
41A3	Carlow	40B1	Dunkettle
38A3	Carrickfergus	38A3	Dunmurry
38B1	Carrick-on-Shannon	39A1	Edgeworthstown
41A2	Carrick-on-Suir	41A3	Enfield (Ireland)
40B1	Carrigaloe	40B3	Ennis
38A1	Castlebar	41A2	Enniscorthy

40A2	Farranfore		38B1	Longford
38A3	Finaghy		39B2	Lurgan
38B2	Fintown		41A3	M3 Parkway
40B1	Fota		39B2	Magheramorne
38A1	Foxford		41B3	Malahide
40A2	Foynes		40B2	Mallow
40A3	Galway		38A1	Manulla Junction
39A3	Giant's Causeway		38A3	Marino
41B1	Glenageary		41A3	Maynooth
38B2	Glenties		40B1	Midleton
40B1	Glounthaune		40A1	Millstreet
39B2	Glynn		38B1	Milltown
41B2	Gorey		39B2	Moira
39B1	Gormanston		41A3	Monesterevan
40B3	Gort		39B1	Mosney
41B1	Grand Canal Dock (3)		38A3	Mossley West
41B3	Graystones		40A2	Moyasta Junction
38A3	Greenisland		41A2	Muine Bheag / Bagenalstown
41A1	Hansfield		41A3	Mullingar
41B1	Harmonstown		39A1	Navan
41A3	Hazelhatch & Celbridge		41A1	Navan Road
38B3	Helen's Bay		40B3	Nenagh
38A2	Hilden		41A2	New Ross
38A3	Holywood		41A3	Newbridge / Droichead Nua
41B1	Howth		39B1	Newry
41B1	Howth Junction		40B3	Oranmore
39B2	Inch Abbey		39A2	Portadown
38A3	Jordanstown		41A3	Portarlington
41B1	Kilbarrack		41A3	Portlaoise
40B1	Kilbarry		41B1	Portmarnock
41A3	Kilcock		39A3	Portrush
41B3	Kilcoole		39B1	Poyntzpass
41A3	Kildare		41B1	Raheny
41A2	Kilkenny		41B3	Rathdrum
40A1	Killarney		40A1	Rathmore
41B1	Killester		38B1	Roscommon
41B3	Killiney		40B3	Roscrea
41A2	Kilmeadan		41B2	Rosslare Europort
31B1	Kiltimagh		41B2	Rosslare Strand
39B2	King Magnus's Halt		41B3	Rush & Lusk
39A1	Kingscourt		40B1	Rushbrooke
41A1	Kishoge		41A3	Sallins & Naas
38A2	Lambeg		41B1	Salthill & Monkstown
41B1	Lansdown Road		41B1	Sandycove & Glasthule
39B2	Larne Harbour		41B1	Sandymount
39B2	Larne Town		39B2	Scarva
39B1	Laytown		38A3	Seahill
41A3	Leixlip Confey		41B1	Seapoint
41A3	Leixlip Louisa Bridge		38B2	Shallogans Halt
40B2	Limerick		41B3	Shankill
40B2	Limerick Junction		40B2	Silvermines
38A2	Lisburn		40B2	Sixmilebridge
40B1	Little Island		39B1	Skerries
39A2	Londonderry (Waterside)		38B1	Sligo

41B1	St. Stephen's Green		40B3	Tuam
41B1	Sutton		41A3	Tullamore
31B1	Swinford		39A3	University (Northern Ireland)
38A3	Sydenham (Belfast)		41A2	Waterford
41B1	Sydney Parade		41A2	Waterford (Bilberry)
39A1	Tara Mines		41A2	Wellington Bridge
41B1	Tara Street (1)		38A1	Westport
40B2	Templemore		41B2	Wexford
38A3	Templepatrick		38A3	Whiteabbey
41A2	Thomastown		39B2	Whitehead
40B2	Thurles		39B2	Whitehead (Excursion Station)
40B2	Tipperary		41B3	Wicklow
31B1	Tobercurry		40B3	Woodlawn
40A2	Tralee (Ballyard)		38A3	York Road Depot
40A2	Tralee (Casement)		38A3	Yorkgate
38A3	Trooperslane		40B1	Youghal

Stations in Britain

55A2	Abbey Road		36A3	Addlestone
52A2	Abbey Wood		37B3	Adisham
25B1	Aber		20A3	Adlington
25B1	Abercynon (9)		20B2	Adlington
25B1	Aberdare		21A3	Adwick
6B1	Aberdeen		43B2	Aigburth
8B1	Aberdour		19B3	Ainsdale
25A3	Aberdovey		43A2	Aintree
18B1	Abererch		1B3	Airbles
25A3	Aberffrwd		1A3	Airdrie
25B1	Abergavenny		52A1	Albany Park
19A2	Abergele & Pensarn		20B1	Albrighton
24B1	Abergwili Junction		20B2	Alderley Edge
19A1	Abergynolwyn		35B3	Aldermaston
33B3	Aberthaw		35B3	Aldershot
25A3	Aberystwyth		54B2	Aldgate
45A2	Abraham Moss		54B2	Aldgate East
15A1	Accrington		36A1	Aldrington
4B2	Achanalt		2B2	Alexandra Parade
4B2	Achnasheen		7B1	Alexandria (5)
4A2	Achnashellach		21A2	Alfreton
13A2	Acklington		55A2	All Saints
23B1	Acle		16A3	Allan's West
47A1	Acocks Green		8B1	Alloa
43B3	Acton Bridge		5A3	Alness
53B2	Acton Central		13A2	Alnmouth (Lionheart)
53B2	Acton Main Line		13A2	Alnmouth for Alnwick
53A1	Acton Town		13A2	Alnwick
47A2	Adderley Park		53A2	Alperton
11A3	Addiewell		29A1	Alresford (Essex)
51B2	Addington Village		35B2	Alresford (Hants)
51A2	Addiscombe		20B2	Alsager

20A2	Bache
25A1	Baglan
25A1	Baglan Bay (20)
35B3	Bagshot
44B1	Bagueley
42A1	Baildon
1B2	Baillieston
54A2	Baker Street
19A1	Bala (Penybont)
36A2	Balcombe
28A2	Baldock
14A1	Baldrine
9B1	Balgreen (4)
51A3	Balham
14A1	Ballabeg
14B1	Ballaglass
14B1	Ballajora
14A1	Ballasalla
14B1	Ballaskeig
7B1	Balloch
14B1	Ballure
9A2	Balmossie
15A1	Bamber Bridge
21A2	Bamford
23A3	Bamforth Street
7B3	Banavie
27A2	Banbury
19A2	Bangor
54B2	Bank
13A3	Bank Foot
43A1	Bank Hall
9A1	Bankhead (6)
50B1	Banstead
10B3	Barassie
54B2	Barbican
21A1	Bardon Hill
12B1	Bardon Mill
15A1	Bare Lane
1A3	Bargeddie
25B1	Bargoed (4)
55B2	Barking
55B3	Barkingside
44B2	Barlow Moor Road
36B3	Barming
19A1	Barmouth
52A1	Barnehurst
53B1	Barnes
53B1	Barnes Bridge
22A3	Barnetby
36A2	Barnham
2B3	Barnhill
21A3	Barnsley
33A2	Barnstaple
26B3	Barnt Green
53B1	Barons Court
1B1	Barrhead
10B1	Barrhill
28B2	Barrington
14B2	Barrow Docks
17A1	Barrow Haven (2)
21A2	Barrow Hill
32A1	Barrow Road, Bristol
14B2	Barrow-in-Furness
21A1	Barrow-upon-Soar
32A2	Barry
32A2	Barry Docks
32A2	Barry Island
9A2	Barry Links
26A2	Barton
45B1	Barton Dock
17A1	Barton-on-Humber (3)
17B3	Basford
28B1	Basildon
35B3	Basingstoke
36B3	Bat & Ball
13A1	Bates
34B3	Bath Spa
8B1	Bathgate
42B2	Batley
16B3	Battersby
54A1	Battersea Park
37A2	Battle
29A1	Battlesbridge
49A3	Bayford
54A2	Bayswater
27B1	Beaconsfield
17B3	Beaconsfield Street
27A2	Bearley
1A1	Bearsden
37A3	Bearsted
7A3	Beasdale
28B1	Beaulieu Park
35A2	Beaulieu Road
5A2	Beauly
43B1	Bebington
29B3	Beccles
51B2	Beckenham Hill
51B2	Beckenham Junction
51A2	Beckenham Road (7)
14B2	Beckfoot
55B2	Beckton
55B2	Beckton Depot
55B2	Beckton Park
52A2	Becontree
16A2	Bedale
19A2	Beddgelert
51A2	Beddington Lane
13B3	Bede

28A2	Bedford
28A2	Bedford St. John's
35B2	Bedhampton (8)
32A1	Bedminster
27A3	Bedworth
35A3	Bedwyn
17B2	Beeston
17B2	Beeston Centre
23B2	Beighton / Drake House Lane
37B3	Bekesbourne
51A2	Belgrave Walk
14B1	Belle Vue (IOM)
45B3	Belle Vue (Manchester)
2B2	Bellgrove
51B3	Bellingham
1B3	Bellshill
50B1	Belmont
21A2	Belper
54A3	Belsize Park
36B3	Beltring
52A2	Belvedere
17A2	Bempton
15B1	Ben Rhydding
44B2	Benchill
29A1	Benfleet for Canvey Island
15A2	Bentham
35B2	Bentley (Hampshire)
21A3	Bentley (South Yorkshire)
13A3	Benton
31A3	Bere Alston
31A3	Bere Ferrers
28A1	Berkhamsted
27A3	Berkswell (1)
54B1	Bermondsey
23B1	Berney Arms
20B3	Berry Brow
50B2	Berrylands
36B2	Berwick
12B3	Berwick-upon-Tweed
19B1	Berwyn
20A3	Bescar Lane
46B3	Bescot Stadium
46B3	Bescot Yards
44A2	Besses-o'-th'-Barn
36A3	Betchworth
54B2	Bethnal Green
19A2	Betws-y-Coed
17A1	Beverley
26B3	Bewdley
36B2	Bexhill
52A1	Bexley
52A1	Bexleyheath
27B1	Bicester North
27B1	Bicester Town

51B2	Bickley
43A1	Bidston
28A2	Biggleswade
46A3	Bilbrook
28B1	Billericay
16A3	Billingham
36A2	Billingshurst
46A3	Bilston Central
21B1	Bingham
42A1	Bingley
27A3	Birch Coppice
32A3	Birchgrove
37B3	Birchington-on-Sea
20A3	Birchwood
51A2	Birkbeck (9)
19B3	Birkdale
43A1	Birkenhead Central
43A1	Birkenhead Hamilton Square (2)
43A1	Birkenhead North
43A1	Birkenhead Park (1)
8B1	Birkhill (6)
23B2	Birley Lane
23B2	Birley Moor Road
46B1	Birmingham Curzon Street
47B1	Birmingham Interchange
47B1	Birmingham International
46B1	Birmingham Moor Street
46A1	Birmingham New Street
46A1	Birmingham Snow Hill
16A3	Bishop Auckland
16A3	Bishop Auckland West (5)
33B2	Bishop's Lydeard
28B1	Bishop's Stortford
2B3	Bishopbriggs
36B1	Bishopstone
1A1	Bishopton
35A2	Bitterne
34A3	Bitton
46B2	Black Lake
15A1	Blackburn
13A1	Blackfell (6)
54B2	Blackfriars (3)
55A1	Blackheath
55A3	Blackhorse Road
51A2	Blackhouse Lane
14B1	Blackpool North
14B1	Blackpool Pleasure Beach
14B1	Blackpool South
8B1	Blackridge
20A3	Blackrod
55A2	Blackwall (2)
35B3	Blackwater
18B3	Blaenau Ffestiniog
8B3	Blair Atholl

Ref	Station
1A3	Blairhill
47A3	Blake Street
46A1	Blakedown
33A2	Blakmoor Gate
1B3	Blantyre
12B1	Blaydon
21B2	Bleasby
27B1	Bledlow Bridge Halt
27B2	Bletchley
19B1	Blodwell
46B3	Bloxwich
20B1	Bloxwich North
33B3	Blue Anchor
43A1	Blundellsands & Crosby
26B1	Blunsdon
13A1	Blyth
20B1	Blythe Bridge
8B1	Bo'ness
5B1	Boat of Garten
37A2	Bodiam
30B3	Bodmin General
30B3	Bodmin Parkway
18B2	Bodorgan
36A1	Bognor Regis
7B1	Bogston
20A3	Bolton
15B1	Bolton Abbey
21A3	Bolton-on-Dearne
54A2	Bond Street
18B2	Bontnewydd
50A1	Bookham
14B2	Bootle (Cumbria)
43A1	Bootle New Strand
43A1	Bootle Oriel Road
46B1	Bordesley
54B1	Borough
36B3	Borough Green & Wrotham (14)
25A3	Borth
30B3	Boscarne Junction
35B2	Bosham
22A2	Boston
22A1	Boston Docks
18A3	Boston Lodge
53A1	Boston Manor
35A2	Botley
21B1	Bottesford
16B3	Boulby
49A1	Bounds Green
27B1	Bourne End
34B1	Bournemouth
34B1	Bournemouth West Depot
47A1	Bournville
27B2	Bow Brickhill
55A2	Bow Church
55A2	Bow Road
49A1	Bowes Park
44A2	Bowker Vale
1A1	Bowling
36A3	Boxhill & Westhumble (11)
27B2	Brackley
35B3	Bracknell
42A1	Bradford Forster Square
42A1	Bradford Interchange
34B3	Bradford-on-Avon
35B1	Brading
42B1	Bradley Jc
46B3	Bradley Lane
42B1	Bradley Wood Jc
29A1	Braintree
29A1	Braintree Freeport
17B2	Bramcote Lane
44B2	Bramhall
42A2	Bramley (Hampshire)
35B3	Bramley (West Yorkshire)
12A1	Brampton (Cumbria)
29B3	Brampton (Suffolk)
23B1	Brampton Halt (Norfolk)
7B1	Branchton
29A3	Brandon
34B1	Branksome
14B3	Braystones
9A3	Brechin
44B2	Bredbury
11A3	Breich
53B3	Brent Cross
53A1	Brentford
52B3	Brentwood
29A3	Bressingham
48A3	Bricket Wood
8A1	Bridge of Allan
9A3	Bridge of Dun
7B2	Bridge of Orchy
2B2	Bridge Street
33A3	Bridgend
2B2	Bridgeton
26A3	Bridgnorth
33B2	Bridgwater
17A2	Bridlington
15B1	Brierfield
22A3	Brigg
42B1	Brighouse
36A1	Brighton
49A2	Brimsdown
44B2	Brinnington
32A2	Bristol Parkway
32A1	Bristol Temple Meads
25B1	Brithdir
16B3	British Steel Redcar

43A1	Conway Park	49A2	Crews Hill
19A2	Conwy	7B2	Crianlarich
36B2	Cooden Beach	18B1	Criccieth
27B1	Cookham	23A3	Cricket Inn Road
36B2	Cooksbridge	26B1	Cricklade
31A3	Coombe Junction Halt	53B3	Cricklewood
51A2	Coombe Lane	2B1	Croftfoot
28B1	Coopersale Halt (12)	55A1	Crofton Park
33A1	Copplestone	23B1	Cromer
12B1	Corbridge	21A2	Cromford
27B3	Corby	1B1	Crookston
34B1	Corfe Castle	42A3	Cross Gates
2A2	Corkerhill	25B1	Cross Keys
14B3	Corkickle	44B2	Crossacres (8)
14B1	Cornaa	42A1	Crossflatts
45B2	Cornbrook	55A1	Crossharbour
7B3	Corpach	2B2	Crosshill
46B1	Corporation Street	2A2	Crossmyloof
7B3	Corrour	20A3	Croston
19B1	Corwen	36B2	Crowborough
32A3	Coryton	33B2	Crowcombe Heathfield
46A3	Coseley	37A2	Crowhurst
20B1	Cosford	21B3	Crowle
35B2	Cosham	35B3	Crowthorne
21B2	Cottam	48A2	Croxley
17A1	Cottingham	48A2	Croxley Green
42A2	Cottingley	1A3	Croy
51A1	Coulsdon South	45A2	Crumpsall
51A1	Coulsdon Town	51A2	Crystal Palace
26B3	Country Park Halt	23B2	Crystal Peaks
23A1	County School	20A2	Cuddington
54B2	Covent Garden	49A3	Cuffley
27A3	Coventry	27A1	Culham
27A3	Coventry Arena	13B3	Cullercoats
2B3	Cowcaddens	5A3	Culrain
36B2	Cowden	1A3	Cumbernauld
8B1	Cowdenbeath	9A2	Cupar
33B1	Cownhayne	8B1	Curriehill
46A2	Cradley Heath	55A2	Custom House
7B1	Craigendoran (4)	55A1	Cutty Sark
16A2	Crakehall	36B3	Cuxton
13A1	Cramlington	25B1	Cwm Bargoed (7)
33B1	Cranbrook	25B1	Cwmbach
34A3	Cranmore	25B1	Cwmbrân
34A3	Cranmore West	25A1	Cwmgwrach
26A3	Craven Arms	24B1	Cwmmawr
36A2	Crawley	19B1	Cyfronydd
52A1	Crayford	25A2	Cynghordy
33A1	Crediton	24B2	Cynwyl Elfed
29A1	Cressing	55B2	Cyprus
43B2	Cressington	52A2	Dagenham Dock
21A2	Creswell	52A2	Dagenham East
20A2	Crewe	52A2	Dagenham Heathway
34A2	Crewkerne	17A1	Dairycoates (1)

13A1	Millfield (7)
1B1	Milliken Park
14B2	Millom
44A2	Mills Hill
42B1	Milner Royd Jc
1A1	Milngavie
20B3	Milnrow
27B2	Milton Keynes Central
33B3	Minehead
18A3	Minffordd
14B1	Minorca
37B3	Minster
42B1	Mirfield
29A2	Mistley
51A2	Mitcham
51A2	Mitcham Eastfields (13)
51A2	Mitcham Junction
44B1	Mobberley
9A2	Monifieth
21A3	Monk Bretton
27B1	Monks Risborough (6)
13B3	Monkseaton
45A3	Monsall
32A2	Montpelier
9B3	Montrose
13A3	Monument
17B3	Moor Bridge
48A2	Moor Park
44B1	Moor Road
43A1	Moorfields
54B2	Moorgate
45A1	Moorside
31A3	Moorswater
21A3	Moorthorpe
4A1	Morar
15A1	Morcambe
33A2	Morchard Road
50B2	Morden (5)
50B2	Morden Road (4)
50B2	Morden South
34B1	Moreton
43A1	Moreton
27A2	Moreton-in-Marsh
19A1	Morfa Mawddach
42B2	Morley
54A2	Mornington Crescent
13A1	Morpeth
27A1	Morris Cowley
35B3	Mortimer
53B1	Mortlake
20A3	Moses Gate (5)
15A1	Moss Side
23B2	Moss Way
44A3	Mossley
43A2	Mossley Hill
1B1	Mosspark
44A2	Moston
1B3	Motherwell
50B2	Motspur Park
51B3	Mottingham
35A2	Mottisfont & Dunbridge
20A2	Mouldsworth
36A1	Moulsecoomb
2B1	Mount Florida
1B2	Mount Vernon
25B1	Mountain Ash (17)
36B2	Mountfield
55A1	Mudchute
5A2	Muir of Ord
2A1	Muirend
14B2	Muncaster Mill
9B2	Murrayfield Statdium
9B1	Musselburgh
15B1	Mytholmroyd
17A1	Nafferton
34A3	Nailsea & Backwell
5A2	Nairn
19A1	Nant Gwernol
18A3	Nantmor
20A2	Nantwich
25A3	Nantyronen
31B3	Nappers Halt
24B1	Narberth
27A3	Narborough
44B1	Navigation Road
53B3	Neasden
25A1	Neath
29A2	Needham Market
1B1	Neilston
15B1	Nelson
43B1	Neston
21B1	Netherfield (7)
23A3	Netherthorpe Road
14B3	Nethertown
35A2	Netley (5)
42A2	Neville Hill
51B1	New Addington
49A2	New Barnet
51B2	New Beckenham
43A1	New Brighton
22A3	New Clee
55A1	New Cross
55A1	New Cross Gate
11A2	New Cumnock
51B3	New Eltham
17A1	New Holland
36B3	New Hythe
45B3	New Islington

7A2	Oban		13B3	Palmersville
35A2	Ocean Terminal		35B3	Pangbourne
52B2	Ockendon		16A1	Pannal
36A2	Ockley		25B1	Pant (Merthyr)
33A1	Okehampton		19B1	Pant (Shropshire)
46B2	Old Hill		25A1	Pantyffynnon
17B2	Old Market Square		30B3	Par
53B2	Old Oak Common		20A3	Parbold
43A2	Old Roan		23A2	Park Grange
54B2	Old Street		23A2	Park Grange Croft
45B2	Old Trafford		42B2	Park Halt
34B3	Oldfield Park		13A1	Park Lane (9)
44A2	Oldham Central		53A2	Park Royal
44A2	Oldham King Street		48A3	Park Street
44A3	Oldham Mumps		30B3	Parkandillack
34A3	Oldland Common		26A1	Parkend
47A1	Olton		34B1	Parkstone
14A1	Onchan Head		33A3	Parracombe
28B1	Ongar		32A1	Parson Street
25A1	Onllwyn		53B1	Parsons Green
37A2	Ore		2A3	Partick
20A3	Ormskirk		44B1	Partington
51B2	Orpington		14B3	Parton
20A3	Orrell		32A2	Patchway
43A2	Orrell Park		45A1	Patricroft
28A3	Orton Mere		1B1	Patterton
53A1	Osterley		35B2	Paulsgrove
19B1	Oswestry		20B2	Peak Forest
36B3	Otford		54B1	Peckham Rye
29B3	Oulton Broad North		44B2	Peel Hall
29B3	Oulton Broad South		13A2	Pegswood
42B2	Outwood		13B3	Pelaw
54B1	Oval		20A3	Pemberton (2)
43B2	Overpool		24B1	Pembrey & Burry Port
35A3	Overton		24A1	Pembroke
15A2	Oxenholme, Lake District		24A1	Pembroke Dock
15B1	Oxenhope		24B1	Penally
27A1	Oxford		32A3	Penarth
54A2	Oxford Circus		33B3	Pencoed
27A1	Oxford Parkway		25B1	Pengam
46A3	Oxley		51A2	Penge East
50A1	Oxshott		51A2	Penge West (11)
51B1	Oxted		25A3	Penhelig
54A2	Paddington		21A3	Penistone
36B3	Paddock Wood		20B1	Penkridge
20A3	Padgate		19A2	Penllyn
27B1	Page's Park		19A2	Penmaenmawr
31B3	Paignton		30B2	Penmere
31B3	Paignton Queen's Park		25B1	Penrhiwceiber (16)
1B1	Paisley Canal		18A3	Penrhyn
1B1	Paisley Gilmour Street		18A3	Penrhyndeudraeth
1A1	Paisley St. James		15A3	Penrith (The North Lakes)
13A1	Pallion		30B3	Penryn
49A2	Palmers Green		19A1	Pensarn

36B3	Penshurst
25B1	Pentre Bach
19A1	Pentrepiod
25B3	Pen-y-Bont
18B1	Penychain
19B2	Penyffordd
18A3	Pen-y-Mount
30A2	Penzance
13B3	Percy Main
53A2	Perivale
30B3	Perranwell
47A2	Perry Barr
26B2	Pershore
8B2	Perth
36A1	Peter Pan's Playground
28A3	Peterborough
28A3	Peterborough Town (11)
35B2	Petersfield
51B2	Petts Wood
36B2	Pevensey & Westham
36B2	Pevensey Bay
35A3	Pewsey
51A2	Phipps Bridge
17B3	Phoenix Park
54A2	Picadilly Circus
45B2	Piccadilly Gardens
16B2	Pickering
29A1	Pig's Bay
26A1	Pilning
54A1	Pimlico
33B1	Pinhoe
48A1	Pinner
8B3	Pitlochry
28B1	Pitsea
27B3	Pitsford & Brampton
55A2	Plaistow
18A3	Plas Halt
19A2	Plas-y-Nant (4)
15A1	Pleasington
46B3	Pleck Jc
4A2	Plockton
37A3	Pluckley
20A2	Plumley
36B2	Plumpton
55B1	Plumstead
31A2	Plym Bridge
31A2	Plymouth
31A2	Plymouth Friary
32A2	Plymouth Road (6)
35A1	Pokesdown
36B2	Polegate
21A1	Polesworth
2A1	Pollokshaws East
2A1	Pollokshaws West
2A2	Pollokshields East
2A2	Pollokshields West
8B1	Polmont
33B1	Polsloe Bridge
45B2	Pomona
49A2	Ponders End
18A3	Pont Croesor
25A1	Pontarddulais
21A3	Pontefract Baghill
16A1	Pontefract Monkhill (6)
42B3	Pontefract Tanshelf
25B1	Pontlottyn (6)
55B2	Pontoon Dock
24B2	Pontprenshitw
25B1	Pontsticill
33B3	Pontyclun
25A1	Pontycymmer
19A2	Pont-y-Pant
25B1	Pontypool & New Inn
25B1	Pontypridd (8)
34B1	Poole
55A2	Poplar (1)
16A1	Poppleton
14A1	Port Erin
7B1	Port Glasgow
14A1	Port Soderick
14A1	Port St. Mary
43B1	Port Sunlight
25A1	Port Talbot Docks
25A1	Port Talbot Parkway
35B2	Portchester
25B1	Porth
18A3	Porthmadog
18A3	Porthmadog Harbour
34A3	Portishead
6B1	Portlethen
46A3	Portobello Jc
36A1	Portslade
35B1	Portsmouth & Southsea
33A2	Portsmouth Arms
35B1	Portsmouth Harbour
32A2	Portway Park & Ride
2A3	Possilpark & Parkhouse
48B2	Potters Bar
14B1	Poulton-le-Fylde
9B2	Powderhall
44B2	Poynton
20A1	Prees
43A2	Prescot
19B2	Prestatyn
20B2	Prestbury
15A1	Preston
36A1	Preston Park
53A3	Preston Road

2B3	Springburn St. Rollox
9A2	Springfield
13A1	Springwell (5)
14B1	Squires Gate
13A1	Stadium of Light
20B1	Stafford
36A3	Staines
21B3	Stainforth & Hatfield
22A3	Stallingborough
44A3	Stalybridge
22A1	Stamford
53B1	Stamford Brook
54B3	Stamford Hill
28B1	Stanford-le-Hope
15B3	Stanhope
43B2	Stanlow & Thornton
48B2	Stanmore
28B2	Stansted Airport
28B2	Stansted Mountfitchet
37A3	Staplehurst
32A2	Stapleton Road
55A2	Star Lane
16A1	Starbeck
33B1	Starcross
17B2	Station Street
15A2	Staveley
31B3	Staverton Bridge
47A2	Stechford
15B1	Steeton & Silsden
54B2	Stepney Green
1A2	Stepps
28A2	Stevenage
10B3	Stevenston
28A2	Stewartby
10B3	Stewarton
8A1	Stirling
44B2	Stockport
21A3	Stocksbridge
12B1	Stocksfield
21A3	Stocksmoor
16A3	Stockton
54B1	Stockwell
33B2	Stogumber
27B1	Stoke Mandeville
54B3	Stoke Newington
20B1	Stoke-on-Trent
20B1	Stone
52B1	Stone Crossing
53A2	Stonebridge Park
36B2	Stonegate
6B1	Stonehaven
27B2	Stonehenge Works
26B1	Stonehouse
50B2	Stoneleigh

46A1	Stourbridge Junction
46A1	Stourbridge Town
12A3	Stow
29A2	Stowmarket
10A1	Stranraer Harbour
55A2	Stratford
55A2	Stratford International
55A2	Stratford Market
27A2	Stratford-upon-Avon
27A2	Stratford-upon-Avon Parkway
4A2	Strathcarron
50B3	Strawberry Hill
51A2	Streatham
51A2	Streatham Common
51A2	Streatham Hill
2B2	Street
42B3	Streethouse
45B1	Stretford
44B3	Strines
4A2	Stromeferry
36B3	Strood
26B1	Stroud
20B3	Stubbins
21A1	Stud Farm (8)
37A3	Sturry
44B2	Styal
29A2	Sudbury
53A3	Sudbury and Harrow Road
53A3	Sudbury Hill
53A3	Sudbury Hill, Harrow
53A2	Sudbury Town
25A2	Sugar Loaf
32A3	Sully Moors
20B3	Summerseat
2A3	Summerston
17B2	Summerwood Lane
50A2	Sunbury
13A1	Sunderland
13A1	Sunderland Docks
51B2	Sundridge Park
36A3	Sunningdale
13A1	Sunniside
36A3	Sunnymeads
50B2	Surbiton
55A1	Surrey Quays
51A2	Sutton
47A3	Sutton Coldfield
50B2	Sutton Common
43A3	Sutton Oak
21A2	Sutton Parkway
37A3	Swale
34B1	Swanage
52A1	Swanley
52B1	Swanscombe

34B3	Westbury	51A1	Whyteleafe South
29A1	Westcliff (3)	21A1	Wichnor Jc
55A1	Westcombe Park	3B1	Wick
37A2	Westenhanger	28B1	Wickford
9A1	Wester Hailes	29B2	Wickham Market
29A2	Westerfield	13A2	Widdrington
34A3	Westerleigh	43A3	Widnes
1A1	Westerton	47B1	Widney Manor
55A2	Westferry	20A3	Wigan North Western (1)
8B1	Westfield (Fife)	20A3	Wigan Wallgate
23B2	Westfield (Sheffield)	23A1	Wighton Halt
37B3	Westgate-on-Sea	11B1	Wigton
20A3	Westhoughton (3)	33A3	Wildmill
54B1	Westminster	17B2	Wilford Lane
34A3	Weston Milton	17B2	Wilford Village
34A3	Weston-super-Mare	17B3	Wilkinson Street
44A2	Westwood	53B2	Willesden Green
12A1	Wetheral	53B2	Willesden Junction
23A1	Weybourne	53A2	Willesden Yards
50A2	Weybridge	2A1	Williamwood
34A1	Weymouth	21A1	Willington
44B3	Whaley Bridge	33B2	Williton
15A1	Whalley	27A2	Wilmcote
34A3	Whatley	44B2	Wilmslow
21A2	Whatstandwell (2)	47B3	Wilnecote
1A3	Whifflet	34B2	Wilton Jc
33B1	Whimple	50B2	Wimbledon
7B1	Whinhill (11)	50B2	Wimbledon Chase (1)
43A2	Whiston	50B3	Wimbledon Park
47B2	Whitacre Jc	26B2	Winchcombe
16B3	Whitby	37A2	Winchelsea
32A3	Whitchurch (Cardiff) (1)	35A2	Winchester
35A3	Whitchurch (Hampshire)	35B3	Winchfield
20A1	Whitchurch (Shropshire)	49A2	Winchmore Hill
53B2	White City	15A2	Windermere
49A1	White Hart Lane	36A3	Windsor & Central
23B2	White Lane	36A3	Windsor & Eton Riverside (10)
29A1	White Notley	35B3	Winnersh
54B2	Whitechapel	35B3	Winnersh Triangle (11)
2A1	Whitecraigs	20A2	Winsford
26A1	Whitecroft	27B1	Winslow
44A1	Whitefield	46B2	Winson Green, Outer Circle (2)
14B3	Whitehaven	21A2	Wirksworth
28B3	Whitemoor	22B1	Wisbech
24B1	Whitland	1B3	Wishaw
13B3	Whitley Bay	29A1	Witham
16A1	Whitley Bridge (8)	44B2	Withington (2)
47A1	Whitlock's End	36A2	Witley
37A3	Whitstable	37A2	Wittersham Road
28A3	Whittlesea	47A3	Witton
28B2	Whittlesford Parkway	36A2	Wivelsfield
50A3	Whitton	29A1	Wivenhoe
21A2	Whitwell	27B2	Woburn Sands
51A1	Whyteleafe	36A3	Woking